To Wilma,

In admiration and
with thanks

All the Noise of It

Living in a Tuscan Hilltown

Christopher H. Warren

ISBN: 978-1-4834-7570-7 (sc)
ISBN: 978-1-4834-7572-1 (hc)
ISBN: 978-1-4834-7571-4 (e)

Library of Congress Control Number: 2017915612

Because of the dynamic nature of the Internet, any web addresses or links contained in this book may have changed since publication and may no longer be valid. The views expressed in this work are solely those of the author and do not necessarily reflect the views of the publisher, and the publisher hereby disclaims any responsibility for them.

Any people depicted in stock imagery provided by Thinkstock are models, and such images are being used for illustrative purposes only. Certain stock imagery © Thinkstock.

Conigliera Press rev. date: 11/24/2017

To my father, Kenneth S. Warren, MD

June 11, 1929–September 18, 1996

We shall not cease from exploration

The Infinite

It was always dear to me, this solitary hill,
And this hedgerow that hides so large a part
Of the far horizon from my view. Sitting and gazing,
In thought I imagine endless space, unearthly silences
And deepest quiet; so for a time
The heart is not afraid. And when I hear
The wind come rustling amongst the leaves
I compare that voice to this infinite silence:
It brings to mind Eternity,
The seasons that are dead, and the living present
And ***all the noise of it.*** So it is
In that enormity my thoughts are immersed,
And foundering is sweet to me in that sea.

—Giacomo Leopardi 1819

Preface

Sorano is a medieval hilltown located above the agricultural plains of the Maremma, a few kilometers from Lazio—the province of Rome—in an area now popularized as "unknown Tuscany." The town is built on a ridge of volcanic rock rising out of the valley of the Lente River. Only the towering fortress, begun in the thirteenth century by the Aldobrandeschi family and added to in later centuries by the Orsini and the Medici, is visible from the surrounding plain. Both the fortress and the town were constructed using blocks of the local ochre-colored magma called *tufo*—or "tuff" in English. Most of the houses in the old town along the principal street, the Via Roma, were the first to be built. In time the town was expanded, with a labyrinth of streets proceeding down the sides of the ridge towards the river on both sides, north and south, forming the various neighborhoods that are still known today as *il Borgo* (the village), *il Poggio* (the hill), or *la Sparna* (the terrace).

The Via Roma ends at the Piazza della Chiesa, where the church of San Niccolò was founded in 1276. I attended a funeral Mass there on November 6, 2016, in honor of Ottorino Savelli, born in Sorano in 1923 to Leonora and Giovanni, and given by the recently arrived town priest, Don Felicien Boduka N'Glandey from the Democratic Republic of the Congo. I knew Ottorino because I occasionally went to his wine cantina at the end of the Via del Ghetto in the old Jewish quarter of Sorano. Some years I helped him with his winemaking, but most often I would simply sit and help him drink his decent white wine—*vino genuino* as a local wine is often referred to in Italy.

In 1988, when I first arrived in Sorano, there were still quite a few men of Ottorino's generation who continued to make wine in their cantinas.

On weekends in particular, I would go on pleasantly tipsy cantina crawls throughout the town, sampling the various wines available. Some years it rained excessively, or the grapes suffered damage from hail. But whatever the state of the grapes, there was no selection: Once harvested they all went into the vats to ferment. In certain cantinas hygiene was not the foremost concern, but it didn't really matter because the wine was made to be consumed within the year. Sometimes the wine would go off a bit and have a vinegary bouquet. To prevent this, modern methods require the use of sodium metabisulfite as a preservative. The popular thinking was that if it said on the packet that one should measure out ten grams per hectoliter of wine, then thirty grams would certainly do the job better—so the overly medicated wine had a decidedly overpowering sulfurous aroma.

Ottorino's wine was slightly sweet but certainly one of the best. I learned well from my tasting experiences, and in a couple of years, I started to make my own wine. Ottorino also provided me with some good advice. In the early nineties, the climate was quite different than today, and it was not unusual for the grapes at maturation to produce only an 11 percent alcohol wine—and that poses preservation problems. Ottorino one day matter-of-factly told me to just add 1.5 kilos of sugar per 100 liters of wine, and I could raise the alcohol content by 1 percent. In a couple of bad growing years, I followed his advice. Nowadays, the summers are hotter and longer, and so the wine gets to 13 percent alcohol without any help.

In his later years, Ottorino had a noticeable limp and eventually went to see a specialist. The diagnosis was water on the knee, to which Ottorino stoutly objected, as he claimed not to drink water—this from a purported five-liter-of-wine-a-day man in his prime. In his final years, Ottorino sold his vineyard and olive grove and stopped going to his cantina. Always eager to raise a glass, even in his nineties, he would make the round of the bars—a rather solitary figure, as his contemporaries were either too infirm to join him or had already passed on.

After the funeral Mass, I joined the mourners as we formed a procession behind the hearse, and we began the long slow walk from the old town to the cemetery on the plain above the Lente River valley. On the way, I stopped off briefly to see Gianni, the newsagent. I had to apologize to him, because I had not yet printed out a description in Italian of the American Cato Institute for which he had asked me. Gianni looks quite like the British actor Terry Thomas, a comic who was famous in the 1950s and 60s, and has the same roguish sense of humor. Previously he worked as a banker and has a keen interest in history and political science. Gianni is also a member of the Mari clan—dyed-in-the-wool Communists who are dismissive of most things American. Although I bought a small apartment from his family, and would often stop at his store to buy newspapers and envelopes, for my first fifteen years in Sorano he would do nothing more than grunt at me. One day he surprised me by disparagingly calling me George. I was rather dismayed by the nickname, but I did not dare respond by calling him Silvio—for the then Italian Prime Minister Berlusconi. Instead, after a while I began to call him Calisto—for the thoroughly disgraced and jailed founder of the Parmalat food conglomerate, Calisto Tanzi. In time we became more friendly, and he began to ask me for simple lessons in conversational English, then for historical information about things such as the NRA—the National Recovery Administration, a New Deal program instituted under Franklin Delano Roosevelt. He was most particularly interested in learning how to pronounce properly the name of the four-term president, but also other figures—some famous, others less known or more notorious. Often I will hear him slowly repeating to himself the names John Kenneth Galbraith, Smedley Butler, and J. Edgar Hoover as I walk by his shop. A sign of our improved relations came when he started calling me Bernie rather than George. He also recently shocked Nadia the bartender by buying me a coffee—she had never before seen him be so generous with anyone.

I posted on my Facebook page photos of Ottorino's death notice and a picture I had taken in the early nineties of him and his long-dead friend Vincenzo Pappalini. In the photo, Vincenzo is waxing lyrical to a pretty friend of mine, and Ottorino looks suitably amused. As a result, I became Facebook friends with one of Ottorino's grandsons from Pisa—Massimiliano. Ottorino was subsequently cremated, and I was invited to the interment ceremony, but unfortunately I had a previous engagement. I sent Massimiliano a message saying that I had instead later gone to Ottorino's favorite bar and drunk a few glasses of wine with friends in his memory. The next time I went to Nadia's bar I was told that Ottorino's son Paolo—father to Massimiliano—was grateful for the friendship I had shown and the attention I had brought to Ottorino, and he had left money for me to have three breakfasts, which I thought was very nice indeed. Nadia was impressed at how many coffees I have been offered of late.

Vincenzo Pappalini (left) Ottorino Savelli (right)

Twenty Novembers ago, in 1996, I made my first visit to the town cemetery, as a member of the funeral procession after the death of Ottorino's first cousin Marietta Savelli. That experience inspired me to write "Where Now Is the Voice," a chapter of this book. When I first began the project, my aim was to animate the abandoned streets of Sorano through the reminiscences of the town's oldest inhabitants. My editor at the time thought the "popular anthropology" too dry, and suggested that I spice up the narrative with "sex and recipes." So I have included some of my escapades, but will leave the recipes for the next book. My experiences bookend the interview section—that remains central to this story of Sorano. I wrote the book in fits and starts—in the 1990s and early 2000s—and have now finished it after a long hiatus. I have decided to leave each section as written, without revision, and I end each one with the original date of completion. So, although I write about Peppina at age sixty-eight as the youngest person I interviewed in the 1990s, she is now the only one of my old friends left alive, and at eighty-six sadly suffers from dementia and is confined to the *casa di riposo*—the old persons' home.

SORANO 2016

Introduction

All the Noise of It begins as the story of an American in a small town in Tuscany. My settling there was due as much to the exotic beauty of the place and a promise of a good quality of life as to my need to escape from modern society that with its apparent freedoms and opportunities, provided me with little faith and no constancy. Ironically, the medieval hilltown's inhabitants, lured by modernity, had abandoned it. Now the modern world's continuing assault on the town's traditional integrity comes in the form of myself and other foreigners.

The idea for this book emerged from the ruins and deserted streets of the "far side" of town, which inspired me to create a traditional-style home and to imagine what life had once been like there. On the far side of town, the past slowly decayed and was reduced to ruins. On the near side, where I have made my home, the past is being increasingly effaced as the few remaining original families move or fade away, and the apartments are transformed into weekend retreats. This book is principally about the dramatic changes that have happened to the town and its inhabitants during the last fifty years. Central to my exploration of the town's past is an account of traditional lifestyles that is based on the recollections of some of the older members of the community.

I had been reluctant to identify the hilltown, as it is still relatively unknown. In fact, the area has been referred to as the "forgotten corner" of Tuscany. *Zolfanello* is an archaic Italian term for a matchstick and is, in fact, an old and apt nickname for the town. "Zolfanello," despite many wars and extended periods of siege, never fell to an opposing force. Indicating its importance during the sixteenth century, Cosimo I of the ruling Medici family termed it "*lo Zolfanello delle guerre in*

Italia"—"the matchstick for Italian wars." As I have heard several times, *"come lo struscai, furono guai."* If you struck them in some way, there was hell to pay. The saying holds true even today as I, rubbing people the wrong way, have suffered through more than a few briefly debilitating explosions. One fellow might respond to my "buon giorno/good day" morning greeting by saying, *"Se era buono non ti avevo incontrato."* If it were good, I would not have bumped into you. Or on another occasion, *"Se era buono, non era per me."* It may have been good, but not for me. Further underscoring the resilient, prickly, and obstinate character of the townspeople, they are well known throughout the region as *capaccioli*—hardheads. Nevertheless, after living here for so many years I'm confident that the capaccioli would not be averse to attention for their town, so I will refer to it by its real name—Sorano. I'm also not afraid of losing any friends. As I have had repeated to me on more than a few occasions, *"A Sorano antico, Se ci campi cent'anni, Non ci farai mai un amico, Pero se ce l'ha fai, Presto o tardi, te ne pentirai.* In Old Sorano, even if you lived to be one hundred, you would never make a friend, but if you did, sooner or later you'd regret it.

The year 1998 was celebrated in Italy as the two-hundredth anniversary of the birth of the poet Giacomo Leopardi, and the title of this book is derived from his poem "The Infinite." I use excerpts and aphorisms from other Leopardi poems, the *Pensieri* or "Reflections on the Character and Behavior of Men in Society," and his notebook—the *Zibaldone*—at the beginning of sections and chapters to highlight themes reflected in the social history of Sorano and to inform my own experiences and ideas. It is humbling to realize that Leopardi died at age thirty-eight, my age at this writing. By twenty-one he had mastered Latin, Greek, Hebrew, and modern European languages. He had done translations of the classics, and written scholarly works on philology and literary criticism. He had completed a third of his vast, rambling, 4526-page compendium of personal notes and thoughts on all manner of disciplines, like philosophy, religion, history, and art, that is the source of ideas for his poems and prose works. He had already published *"L'Infinito"* and other poems that established his place as one of the great poets of the nineteenth century.

Most of Leopardi's youth was spent in solitary intense study, thought to be the cause of his considerable infirmities. Even as a young man he was frail, his eyesight was poor, and he was badly hunchbacked. He was terribly embittered by his physical condition, perhaps mostly because it meant that his love for women could be nothing more than an esoteric contemplation of them. In his darkest, most nihilistic moments he would write, as he did in his late poem "To Himself,"

And to no purpose
Were all your stirrings; earth not worth your sighs.
Boredom and bitterness is life; and all the rest nothing;
the world is dirt.

Yet, from this mortal suffering emerged transcendent images and expressions. One of Leopardi's fundamental ideas is that imagination and hope are the wellsprings of happiness. In the *Zibaldone* he wrote: "Infinite pleasure, that one cannot find in reality, one finds thus in imagination, from which spring hopes and illusions." A few pages later: "The penalty of man in experiencing a pleasure is to see immediately the limits of its extent...because all the good things seem beautiful and sublime from afar, and the unknown is more beautiful than the known...The spirit must naturally prefer to all others that pleasure it cannot embrace."

It is poignant that Leopardi apparently could not appreciate some of the small pleasures of life, but if he had, he likely would never have written "The Infinite." My life would be poorer if I could not enjoy cycling on the winding roads in the beautiful hills above Sorano, stomp the grapes to make my wine, do the hard labor of building and renovation, and have real physical relationships with my loves.

I first arrived in Sorano in 1988. In the twelve years since then, I have slowly renovated my home, learned to speak the local Italian dialect, and have become deeply involved in traditional town activities. In the process, my view of the town and my general idea for the book have been colored and changed. I had originally thought of the book as a paean to a lost way of life, but my experiences have hardened me. As an American, but also simply as a "*forestiere*"—an outsider—I have had considerable struggles. Leopardi wrote that "in human communities nature herself decrees that any man who is very different from most other men...should by every effort be destroyed or chased away." He advised the outsider to remain as anonymous as possible and "to strive to keep your financial state a secret, so that the public should not know whether to despise you or get rid of you and so that you will be treated like most other men." But as an aloof visitor I would never have been able to complete the renovation of my home, or come to an understanding of the people and place. I likely would have left long ago. In addition, my professional career was based on quick investigations, and short trips, with rare opportunities for considered study. I had learned that a snapshot, or even a documentary film, can give only superficial representations of a story, history, or place.

SORANO 2000

The human race, and any small portion of it, is divided into two kinds: the bullies and the bullied. Neither law or power, nor progress of philosophy or civilization, can prevent a man, born or yet to be born, from being one or the other; it remains up to the person to choose, although not everyone is capable of making that choice.

PENSIERI 38[1]

My first visit to Italy came after an arduous trip to India. I had gone to India to photograph the plight of the urban poor. Ostensibly because of Hindu religious law, many of the most destitute—the untouchables—have no means of advancing themselves. Their horizons extend from one side of the filthy streets where they live in their sorry cardboard-and-plastic homes, to the other. Through no fault of their own they are doomed to short lives of misery. From a brief stay in Agra I have retained impressions frozen like photographs. Late one night I had wandered into a slum. I became lost in its dark labyrinths, my way lit by trash fires that illuminated stygian scenes: two small children playing in a gutter's refuse; a man with palsied and damaged limbs wildly askew.

I had a few days of photographic work in northern Italy and decided to extend my visit. My first destination was the Campo de' Fiori in Rome, where in 1600 Giordano Bruno was burned at the stake as a heretic. A casualty of religious fundamentalism, Bruno was an early exponent of a humanist conception of history. His writings were an effort to free the mind and spirit from the stultifying constraints of the predominant worldview of the Church of Rome. I arrived at the Campo de' Fiori at the end of a market day. Wooden stalls lay dismantled, and the ground was littered with refuse, vegetables and flowers trodden underfoot. Bruno's monument is in the middle of the square, and I approached it from behind. On arriving at the statue, I found two young men lying prostrate at its feet. The rain was falling onto their upturned faces, their eyes wide open and uncomprehending, one still with a

---

[1] Leopardi's *Pensieri* are 111 reflections that were published posthumously.

needle in his arm. The image was as strong as any I had encountered in India, but the predicament the two were experiencing contrasted starkly with the brutish lives that so many helpless souls suffer on India's streets. The two drug addicts likely were well educated, perhaps even from privileged backgrounds. If they were not already dead, they were effectively destroying their lives. It was terribly ironic that they had fallen at a monument to a man who had begun to broaden the narrow metaphysical horizons of his day. Their horizons could not have been more blurred or contracted. Their eyes, open yet not seeing even the street before them, could no longer lead them from their abject state. Unlike their Indian counterparts, these men were not the products of religious dogma and political myopia but the results of a permissive society and their own fallibility.

Up to that point in my early career, I had sought out and documented the plight of the hopeless, traveling from the open sewers of Cité Simone in Haiti to the claustrophobic shantytowns of the City of Joy in Calcutta, the reeking garbage dumps of Guatemala, and the AIDS-decimated villages of Uganda. I was observing people who had no choices. Perhaps hypocritically, I could spend the day with a family barely surviving in a Guatemala City dump and that same evening enjoy a drink in luxurious surroundings with someone who would never even consider that family's plight. If the going got rough in India, I could always check into a comfortable hotel, or soothe my sensibilities with a visit to the Taj Mahal.

My interest in the Third World stems in part from my father's research on tropical diseases, which led to my life in a variety of developing countries, beginning at the age of one. As a child I became sensitized to poverty and hopelessness, but the traveling affected me in other ways as well. Rarely, for instance, did I see my American or British grandparents. This peripatetic childhood and isolation from a broader family undermined any strong sense of place and home. From my travels I would return to my apartment in a slowly gentrifying slum in New York's East Village. There I paid a premium to live in a dark closet with a window onto a sooty airshaft. Most of the twenty-four apartments in the building were filled with immigrants and the poor who had no way out. I was able to leave my tenement house, which was strewn with crack vials and condoms and plagued by burglary, assault, and arson, as my purview and opportunities seemed much broader. Yet I found it difficult, when faced with the luxury of choice, to decide firmly what course to pursue in life. In short, at that point I was drifting, without roots.

About this time, I went again to Italy to visit friends in Tuscany. I arrived in Rome early one morning. Unlike the gray drizzly February I had encountered a few years before, this September day was hot and bright. I chose to return to the Campo de' Fiori and have lunch outside one of the restaurants that ring the market, before catching a bus out of the city late that afternoon. I sat, ate a simple pasta, and drank a half liter of good red wine while watching hundreds of people milling amidst the open stalls as they chose from the bountiful displays of fresh flowers, fruit, and vegetables. However, despite the tantalizing and intoxicating presence of people, sun, wine, and color, I could not dispel my unease at the looming sight of the oxidized bronze bulk of Bruno at the center of the lovely tumult.

Thinking inevitably of those two men at Bruno's feet, I began again to consider their predicament. I thought of the addicts' fall, despite the safety nets of the considerable Italian welfare state and the strong kinship networks of the legendary Italian *famiglia*. With all the possibilities of success in a land of beauty, plenty, and the world's greatest cultural heritage, they had abnegated their extraordinary advantages for easy delusions and self-destruction. Of all the destitute people I had observed in the world, I had the most in common with the two Romans. Being healthy and having the possibilities that came from my status, race, and country, I could make decisions, overcome my problems, and get on with my good life.

SORANO 1990

All men, at least in some circumstances...believe extraordinary the events of history and ordinary the stories of fiction.

ZIBALDONE 1903[2]

Sorano's modest museum of medieval history is in a part of the fortress that was built by the ruling Aldobrandeschi family in the thirteenth century. The first exhibit in the museum is a simple view and ground plan of the town. Dating from the 1740s, the original drawing is attributed to Edward Warren. It is sometimes remarked upon in town that I share his last name. The suggestion that he is an ancestor of mine usually is met with skepticism. In both French and Italian, Warren wrote a brief description of the town of Sorano and its castle:

> It is situated above a promontory...with access made more difficult because of the high precipices in many places...The town is surrounded by solidly constructed walls, and is well populated. An excellent wine is cultivated in the surrounding area, and there is a very deep wine cave excavated in the tufo rock that remains so cold that it seems frozen even at the height of summer. It is said that the air is so dense in this cave that the shot of a musket fired from the door has never reached the bottom, even though the distance is not so great.

Known by his Italianized name, Odoardo Warren was from 1739 until his death in 1760 the "Colonel of the Artillery Battalion and Director General of the Fortifications of Tuscany." His considerable duties were to supervise Tuscany's extensive system of fortresses and maintain military readiness. Warren received his military training in France and subsequently served under Francis Stephen, the duke of

---

[2] The numbers refer to the page numbers of Leopardi's original manuscript of the *Zibaldone*.

Lorraine. After the War of the Polish Succession, and by the terms of the 1738 Treaty of Vienna, Francis Stephen was granted Tuscany in exchange for Lorraine. The new Granduca di Toscana, Francesco Stefano di Lorena, succeeded four hundred years of Medici family rule. Married to the Hapsburg empress Maria Theresa of Austria, Francesco Stefano later was named Francis I, emperor of the Holy Roman Empire. He had sixteen children with Maria Theresa. A son, Leopold, succeeded his father as grand duke of Tuscany, oversaw a period of growth and prosperity, and is remembered by a monument in Sorano: the *Masso Leopoldino*. A daughter, Marie Antoinette, became the queen of France.

Other foreigners preceded Edward Warren to Sorano. The Englishman Guy de Montfort, son of the earl of Leicester, was the first husband of Countess Margherita Aldobrandeschi. She went on to marry five times, and the 450-year Aldobrandeschi dynasty, which at times ruled over a considerable part of central Italy, ended at her death in 1313. In 1271 Guy de Montfort avenged the death of his father by murdering his cousin, Henry of Almain, in a church in the nearby papal city of Viterbo. Because of his fall into disgrace, Guy's marriage to Margherita was annulled and Dante put him up to his neck in the Phlegethon, a river of boiling blood in the seventh circle of Hell.

A view of Sorano by Odoardo Warren

Having often changed my abode where I stayed for longer or shorter periods, either months or years, I realized that I was never content, never felt centered, never settled in any place, however excellent it was, until I had some memories to attach to it, to the rooms in which I lived, and to the streets and houses I visited.

ZIBALDONE 4286

I very nearly did not make it to the town that was to become my home or locate the friend who lured me there. After lunch with Giordano Bruno, I did as my friend had instructed and went to the Piazza Esedra in Rome, where I could buy a bus ticket to Tuscany. I found the ticket office within the semicircular arcade, or exedra, which gave the square its original name. I stood for a long while on line, and when I eventually got to one of the three booths I plainly stated to the man behind the glass partition, *"Un biglietto per Sorano."* *"Non c'e,"* he replied. I slowly repeated my destination, thinking that my pronunciation was poor. Again he said, "There is no such place." I wrote the name of the town on a scrap of paper. *"Non esiste."* I went out of the office, stood under the portico, gazed onto the dry Fountain of the Naiads, and considered my options. I was tempted simply to walk the few hundred meters to the Stazione Termini, Rome's main train station, and hop a train south to Naples. Naples was the birthplace of Giordano Bruno, and also that of the great eighteenth-century philosopher of history, Giambattista Vico.

In college one of my particular interests was James Joyce. I wrote a thesis on the influence of Vico's *Scienza Nuova* (*The New Science*) on Joyce's writing, which resulted in my attending a Vico symposium in Dublin in 1982—the hundredth anniversary of Joyce's birth—during the annual Bloomsday celebration. While there, I met some considerable cultural luminaries and went on a challenging pub crawl with the novelist Anthony Burgess and the composer John Cage. Joyce lived in Trieste for more than ten years, and I had already made pilgrimages to the other cities where he resided, Paris and Zurich. So Trieste to the north seemed like a good place to go, too. However, as I am both cynical and relatively indefatigable (qualities that have served me well), I decided to return to the ticket office.

For a second time I stood in line for what must have been half an hour. When my turn came, the booth available was with the same man as before, so I let the person behind me go to him—and the next person as well. At another booth I again made my request, and the amiable lady, with nary a pause, responded "*subito*"—immediately—and pushed a small blue ticket under the window, for which I paid seven thousand lire. The meandering hundred-mile journey took nearly five hours, and when I arrived in Sorano it was the middle of the evening.

The August crowds had left, but the piazza was filled with people standing and chatting or circling in groups arm in arm around a line of plane trees that form its center. Shortly after getting off the bus, I asked a genial man for directions to my friend's address. He wrung his hands, concentrated, and acknowledged that he knew the street, but then rather oddly suggested that I take a road that appeared to lead out of town. I did as he said, but I soon found myself stumbling on a descending road with sharp turns and high walls that made it very dark. When I came to a bridge that went over a river, I decided to turn back. After the ten-minute stroll, I noticed that some young kids were badgering my guide, but I soon happened upon my friend at one of the piazza's three bars. We had a glass of local *vino genuino*, probably quite like that which Edward Warren enjoyed, and then walked down to the historic heart of the town, through an impressive archway. After a few hundred yards, the narrow winding streets brought us to his small apartment, and I soon went to sleep.

By daylight I was able to see the beauty of the town's situation. From the window of the apartment, I looked over terracotta rooftops down to a small verdurous valley. The meandering Lente River runs around the perimeter of the steep crag of porous volcanic tufo on which the town was built. Sorano is a classical medieval hilltown, the houses seeming to grow organically out of and conform to the crag, each four- to five-story structure made of blocks of the earthy red/yellow tufo. Many of the houses date to the twelfth century, although the foundation is pre-Etruscan. A large part of the town is uninhabited, half having been totally abandoned in the 1950s, which lends it an air of exquisite decay.

Bronze-Age and Etruscan caves dot the now wild landscape that had once been thoroughly terraced and cultivated. Much of the town lies below the level of the surrounding plain, so the far hills and precipices of the valley obscure the horizon. Initially for me, the intimacy of the landscape was almost claustrophobic, but I now appreciate it for the security it provides and the limitations it implies.

During my brief first visit I learned that there was a 400-square-foot apartment for sale. Consisting of three small rooms, it had been in the owner's family for generations. He and his brothers and sisters were all born there. The first room, which one entered from the street by walking down four worn-smooth travertine marble steps, was the kitchen. There was a stone sink without running water, a fireplace with a simply carved and thickly painted dark chestnut mantle, and a yellowed, painted poplar cabinet set into the wall opposite the sink. On a square, worm-eaten pine table lay a mound of Socialist Party paraphernalia, and pinned up on one wall was a large red Soviet Social Realist–style poster of marching workers. The walls and wood ceiling of the dark, smoky room had originally been whitewashed. Light came from a barred window looking onto the street and from the opposite wall, where a glass plate was set above a door that led to one of the two bedrooms. One bedroom was painted a pastel pink, and the other a pastel blue, the paint flaking from the beams and boards. Both rooms contained metal bed frames and had windows looking to the far hills. After some haggling over the price, I decided to buy.

The pending transfer of property to an American apparently was a popular topic of conversation, but only after I signed the deed was I admonished by grumbling townspeople for having paid, depending on the speaker, ten to a hundred times as much as any sane person should. Considering that I had purchased a medieval home with its heavy-beamed ceiling, terracotta tile floors, and lovely view for the amount I paid annually to live in my tiny dark tenement-house closet in New York, I reckoned that I had done very well. Especially as apartments similar to mine now command considerable sums because of the town's gradual discovery, largely by Romans and Florentines. Today, the price I paid is considered so low that the previous owner claims, with an avuncular air, that he gave me the apartment as a gift. When I bought the apartment, he was president of the town's Socialist Party. Although most of the Socialists now meet under the banner of the Forza Italia party, and in a grander setting, the impropriety of a young American coming to the town and buying the headquarters of its governing party has not been forgotten.

Only very slowly did I begin to renovate the apartment. Somehow I envisioned simply cleaning the six-centuries-old oak-and-chestnut ceiling, patching the crumbling plaster, introducing a toilet, polishing the brass doorknobs, and moving in. Having accomplished the easy first task of knocking out the flimsy three-quarter-inch-thick tile dividing walls and creating one large light room, it became harder to imagine that those small quarters had housed seven people only thirty-five years before.

Although I have gained an enormous appreciation for the town and its people in my subsequent thirteen years in Sorano, I have also undergone a slow process of disenchantment. Initially I was attracted by a romantic exterior—an ancient place beautiful in its decay. The town, in fact, is abandoned and dilapidated. Only fifty years ago, as many as four thousand people lived there; now there are only two hundred year-round residents. While I love wandering the empty streets, aside from the busy August and the religious holidays, I know that the few old people who still are interested in their old town are saddened to see it deserted.

After a water pipe burst in the late 1950s, a sinkhole appeared in a small piazza on the far side of town, and so began an abrupt and irreversible change for the town and its people. More for reasons of expediency than for the minimal danger the sinkhole posed, half of the town was condemned and a new town was built with financial help from the government. Although there were a few trappings of modernity, most people did not have plumbing, washed their clothes at the river, and basically lived as generations had before them. The people eagerly abandoned their centuries-old, cramped, cold, and humid dwellings for the new suburban-type apartment blocks, devoid of character but with modern conveniences. A slower exodus has been ongoing from the side of town where I live, and only a handful of the generation that was first given the option to leave now remain. Many did not stop at the new town, going on to the greater opportunities afforded by the cities and the world beyond. While the town went to the city, the city has now come to the town, to sometimes bad and sometimes paradoxical effect: One townsman, my age, has succumbed to AIDS, another has had a sex change.

I have been fascinated by the far side of town, and have spent a lot of time there considering the past and gaining inspiration from what I could discern of it. Forty years of rain and wind, freezing and thawing, have taken their toll, and despite occasional attempts at shoring up walls, many of the buildings have fallen in on themselves. With the recent great demand for and dramatically increased value of old tiles, doors, and fireplaces, nothing remains but occasional intact rooms, bare walls, fallen beams and boards, rubble and weeds. Although it was difficult to imagine what life was like as I stood among the ruins, soon the walls and ceilings provoked a change in my thinking about my own home.

Like most people who have come from the outside to create a weekend or holiday retreat, I envisioned my house with white walls and an exposed wooden beam ceiling. But, in fact, as I came to realize from my excursions to the far side of town, homes were traditionally painted with colored lime, both walls and ceilings. Every room of every apartment had been painted with pastel greens, yellows, blues, or pinks. Some were more elaborate than others, with blue walls and pink ceilings for instance, but all were further decorated with elegant thin lines delineating color or breaking the monotony of one color. At the base of the walls, a darker color was employed to hide scuffs and marks caused by shoes and brooms. The lime was not only decorative; its use on the ceilings helped to prevent termite and woodworm infestations. From what I have been told, and from my own observations as I picked away at the many layers of colored lime, homes had been painted this way for centuries, and the simple decorative elements of line and borders suggest an Etruscan origination. So inspired, I chose to create a home in the old style.

Today I have not yet polished the brass doorknobs, but I have almost completed the larger enterprise. Although the floor was weak in only one small area, the owner of the apartment below mine insisted that we redo the entire floor. This meant that I had to remove the floor tiles and a foot of ancient rubble bedding that lay between the tiles and the planking, and then finally chainsaw and pull out the centuries-old beams. As I suspected, although woodworm had superficially consumed the exposed exterior, the centers of the beams and the ends in the walls were rock hard and could have easily borne the weight of another few centuries. A new cement floor was set and poured to strict anti-earthquake specifications, and the old tiles laid on top.

Cleaning and re-stuccoing the ceiling may have been the most unpleasant and time-consuming phase of the restoration. I spent weeks scraping away old paint, removing patches of dry rot, and treating for woodworm infestation. I then had to replace some thoroughly rotten boards, re-stucco between all the boards, and reshape and smooth the exterior of the beams. A sandblaster could have done the cleaning in a day, but I was afraid it might do too much damage to the ancient ceiling, and the cost was excessive. I also removed all the old plaster, and replastered using a mixture of volcanic ash and lime. Described by Vitruvius in his first-century BC *Ten Books on Architecture*, and used by the Etruscans for centuries before his time, the locally available materials are only now being eschewed by builders for expensive modern premixed products. By knocking away the old plaster, I discovered a lovely niche with a travertine arch, and a closed-up doorway, which revealed the way into the next—and larger—apartment, which I was to acquire the following year. My expansion did not stop there: In time I bought yet another apartment, so that my first room is now one of seven in a much larger home.

The other rooms have all gone through similar renovations. I not only wanted to but was, in fact, forced to do most of the work myself, so I have spent far more time in the town than originally planned. As a holiday retreat, the town for me could have simply been a superficial idyll. With time came a real, sometimes sobering, and often amusing understanding of the people and place.

In some places, between civilization and savagery, such as Naples, for example, it can be observed more than elsewhere something that somehow occurs in all places: that is that a man who is reputed to be penniless is not considered a man; believed to be wealthy, he is in danger of his life. Therefore it is necessary in such places, and indeed is generally the custom, to attempt to keep your finances a secret, so that the public should not know whether to despise you or kill you, and so that you will be treated like most other men: partly despised and partly respected, sometimes harmed and sometimes left in peace.

PENSIERI 35

Michele, a former Communist mayor of the town and now a wizened denizen of the Socialist Party–aligned bar, has always been friendly and provided me with quick advice and help. Unfortunately, for my first year or so in Sorano, because of his strong regional accent and slight lisp, I had no idea what he was saying to me. Aware of some of the problems I had in the town, he explained a fundamental hypothesis about the relationship between Italians and Americans. Italians are thieves, he said, as I sipped an early morning cappuccino with him at the bar, but it is the Americans' fault because during the war they came with so much money that they had to be ripped off—and where did they get their money anyway?

A few days later I was able to support Michele's opinion of Italians by quoting from an editorial written by Umberto Eco in one of the newspapers. According to Eco, the Italian character is such that it knowingly permitted the corrupt and now thoroughly discredited ruling coalition of Christian Democrats and Socialists to continue for so long because dishonesty and corruption are the accepted ways of surviving in Italian society. This, of course, prompted a heated discussion among the gathered Socialists. Nadia, the bartender, had the last word on the matter. Poggiolini, the notorious Socialist who embezzled billions of lire from Italy's healthcare system, did right, she said with a straight face, except that he carelessly let himself be exposed.

Then there was Leopoldo, a Communist and one of nine relatives from whom I bought two small rooms. After traveling by hitchhiking, by bus, by bicycle, and on foot all over the province, and after a great deal of coaxing and diplomacy, I managed to get eight of the family to agree to sign the deed. The last obstacle was a cantankerous brother of Leopoldo, from whom I was advised to conceal that I am an American. According to the Communists, the despised opposition was kept in power only because of dollars and the CIA, all part of the Americans' depraved campaign for capitalistic hegemony. Apparently, the brother also abhorred Americans because of a supposed bombing raid that occurred after the Italian government had capitulated at the end of the Second World War. Among the innocent picnicking victims of this mythical American atrocity was a relative of the family. Whether these were the reasons for his disdain, or Leopoldo was concerned that the brother might hold out for more money knowing my country of origin, or in fact it was just an elaborate excuse for his general ill humor, I never found out. With him I claimed my half-English heritage and eventually managed, to many people's surprise, to get all the feuding members of the family into the same room for the signing of the deed.

Gullible, rich, ripe for the plucking, and owner of half of the town, an American had arrived and bought three apartments that had previously housed as many as eight people each. Particularly for the older inhabitants, I and my "kingdom" were a source of resentment, and it has taken time, and certain misadventures, before these opinions could be changed.

In the beginning, the prejudices, my rudimentary grasp of Italian, and my ignorance of local building methods and materials caused me many problems. To be able to plaster the first apartment, I ordered a half ton of volcanic ash—*pozzolana* as it is called—to be delivered to a field outside of town. I then arranged for a tractor and dumpster small enough to navigate the narrow streets of the town down to the apartment. As we were shoveling the ash into the dumpster, the tractor owner expressed some reservation about the quality of the pozzolana, but he did not seem overly concerned. After three trips, we had filled a storage room opposite the apartment. A builder stopped by and cheerfully asked me what I was planning to do with all the dirt. So I rehired the tractor and hauled the dirt out of town to a location where I received permission to dump it.

As I have done so much renovation, the acts of bringing in materials and removing rubble have been numerous, costly, and in this particular case rather torturous. I reordered the pozzolana from another supplier, and made a point of being in the field when it was delivered. This was white pozzolana, he explained as he quickly emptied the truck, and he was willing to give me a good deal on it. Somewhat disgruntled, because I thought pozzolana should be either black or red, I went in search of advice from another builder. He assured me that it was fine, and I subsequently used it for the plaster. After a few months, it cracked and began to fall off the walls. I removed what remained and began the process again. Because of growing despair and lack of time, I hired two men to plaster the second time around. The job was done while I was out of town, and when I returned, the spectacle of poorly finished and cracked and crumbling plaster was demoralizing. The next time around I did the plastering myself, with the correct mixture of materials, and now demonstrate it to my builder friends as a rare example of plaster that is solidly affixed and without cracks.

Even after experiences such as these, I had not yet learned the lesson that if I could not do all the work of restoration myself, I would have to be around to oversee the work of others. In addition, I was eager not to offend, too trusting, and ignorant of the profligate and artful custom of dissembling, so I was marked as a soft touch. As I wised up, the lengths to which certain people went to teach me about the nature of mankind became increasingly exaggerated.

During one stay in town, I devoted my energies to renovating the place I had bought from Leopoldo and family. The floors of this small two-room apartment were dangerously unsafe, so as in the first apartment, I gingerly pulled up the floor and replaced the rotten and not particularly old poplar beams. Norman, a poet visiting from New York, managed to help for half a day before he fell through the floor. He escaped injury, but with him and a couple of others I learned that it was better not to rely on friends when doing renovation.

Most of the roof had been replaced recently, using cement beams, so I chose to put up a false ceiling and, in the process, insulated the roof and enlarged a tiny skylight. I ran pipes for plumbing, bringing water to a sink in the main room and to the small area I had marked out as the bathroom. The bathroom and a narrow bedroom are reached by walking down three steps. In the bedroom I was able to fit a monk's bed, which I was to sleep in for years while renovating the rest of my property. I knocked away most of the old plaster and chiseled out tracks for the plastic tubing in which I eventually ran the electric wiring. I brought in another half ton of pozzolana for the new plaster...and ran out of time.

In the meantime I became friendly with a local builder who was working in a nearby apartment. Most days, we would have espressos together after lunch, and sometimes a beer at the *birreria* in the evening. He impressed me with his cheerful gregariousness, and particularly with his concern for the old people in town. He always had a kind word for the pair of diminutive nonagenarian lovers who had found each other in the retirement home, or a joke for the rotund, eccentric, and invariably pickled "Churchill." Pronounced "Chorchi," he did indeed look like the great prime minister. Apparently, there was also an "Itla," but he died before I came to the town. What I also liked about the builder was that he seemed conscientious and able to do good work.

I engaged him to finish removing the old plaster and create an arch for the then low entrance to the room down the steps. I further asked him to put up a brick wall for the bathroom, redo the small four-square-meter roof above it, hook up the sewer, rebuild the base of the lovely fifteenth-century stone fireplace in the larger room, and retile the floor. We agreed on the price, and he asked that I pay him three-quarters up front. I did this only because he pleaded penury, has a child to feed and educate, etc., and because I liked him.

Perhaps I should not have been surprised when I returned to town and saw what he had wrought. The plaster was severely cracked and falling away in the places where he had not removed the old material. He did not use the pozzolana I had left him but brought in some other product for the plastering. The bathroom wall was well out of plumb, and the hole left for the door strangely distorted. The small roof was leaking grievously. Instead of building the arch as I had asked, he simply put in two reinforced concrete beams at throat level, so that I had to stoop to get into the bedroom. One of those beams extended into a wall cabinet that he had also filled liberally with broken tile and hardened cement. Perhaps to convince me that these were acts of ill will rather than extraordinary incompetence, his crowning offense was to lay, in the main room, half of the expensive old floor tiles upside down.

This stay was very short, as I had to return to work in New York sooner than I had planned, so I did not have time to discuss adequately with the builder my amazement at his work. He showed no inclination to redress even the glaringly obvious problems, and demonstrated a sharp, feral aggressiveness, with his thinned lips and narrowed black eyes, when he asked for the remainder of his fee. I left dismayed and nonplussed by the situation.

When I arrived in New York a few days later, I listened in disbelief to two poisonous messages from the builder on my answering machine. I had not said that I would not give him the balance of his estimate, as I was still weighing my options: to pay and avoid distasteful scenes, or not pay and likely never be able to hire a helper again. "You had better wire me the money," he hissed into the answering machine, or he would return to the rooms and "intervene." Furious, I wrote a letter detailing the atrocious work he had done, explaining that I had no intention of paying him another lira and that if any harm ever came to my house I would go straight to the authorities with the recording of his message.

Returning by bus some time later, and already stressed out by a documentary film trip in Yemen during the Gulf War, I immediately saw the builder at the far end of the piazza. Fully prepared for battle, and rather looking forward to it, I marched up to him. Confounding my expectations, he could not have been more solicitous. "How was your trip?" he inquired pleasantly. "Could I come down and discuss the situation with you tomorrow?"

He arrived as I was sanding down the reversed floor tiles, attempting to make them look more uniform. (Despite three days of effort, the floor still looked terrible, and I have now covered the ruined half with a carpet.) He obsequiously knocked at the open door, came in, and then patiently explained how much more work he had done over the estimate. I firmly showed him that he had in fact done no more than he was originally asked to do, and what he had done he had done badly. After we had senselessly restated our positions for a good two hours, he refused to leave. Eventually, I had to let him know bluntly what I thought of him, using well-suited Italian phrases, some of which I had learned from him. "*Sei uno stronzo. Tu mi hai preso in giro e tutti lo sanno. Non mi rompere i coglioni e va fare un culo!*" You piece of shit, you have taken me for a ride and everyone in town knows it, so stop busting my balls and get fucked! Throughout my harangue he remained strangely impassive, but then suddenly resorted to his final desperate ploy. Tears welled up in his eyes. "My debts, my wife, my child," he pleaded. Overwhelmed by the concluding act of this bravura performance, I gave up and paid him half. I still see the builder often, and we will have an espresso together, occasionally referring amusedly to "the discussion."

The other reason for my short visit was to complete the deed on my wine cantina, which I had arranged to purchase about a year earlier. The cantina lies in the same cul-de-sac as most of my other property. I had fantasies of buying it not only so that I could own all the property at the end of the lane, but also because I wanted one day to make wine. The owner of the cantina was Ermanno, a man in his late seventies who always reminded me of a gentle bear—large, deliberate, and sometimes ponderous. I usually saw him playing cards with his pensioner cronies at the Communist bar. Occasionally he would come down to the cantina to drink wine, or perhaps some of his famous fruit-flavored grappa, with one of his friends. I always apologized to him because I was making a terrible noise with my angle grinder or had created a thick cloud of plaster dust, but he would remain amiably unfazed. One day I decided to ask him to sell me the cantina, and he surprised me by assenting immediately. We wrote up a legally binding private agreement in which it was stipulated that I pay a deposit and that, over a period of three years, I would pay at intervals until I reached the fair price. Ermanno was very kind to agree to the installment plan, particularly as the dollar was at that time at a low against the lira.

Soon thereafter, Ermanno appeared at the door as I was eating my lunch. With a hard expression, he asked to see my copy of our agreement. He snatched it from my hand, shoved it in his pocket, and demanded that I pay my outstanding debt to him, plus a series of fictitious taxes that added up to a considerable sum. Flabbergasted, I tried to reason with him, explaining that I simply did not have the money.

Unfortunately, Ermanno had obviously been listening to his friends, the myth of the rich American again proving more persuasive than reality. He became quite unpleasant and growled that if I did not pay him, he would take the keys away and no longer sell me the cantina. Although I could easily have prevailed legally, I decided to avoid the hassle, scrounged up the necessary dollars, exchanged them at the terrible rate, and paid him the total original sum for the property.

When I came to sign the deed, I knew that Ermanno was waiting for me to cough up his additional imaginary sum. I arranged the meeting with the notary for the day following my arrival from New York (the same time that I discovered the terrible job the tearful builder had done), and I hoped to avoid seeing Ermanno before then. But at six in the morning, there was a fearful banging at the door. Jet-lagged and not knowing quite where I was, I did not respond immediately. It was Ermanno, and he began to pound harder and started yelling at the top of his lungs: "Filthy vagabond, American pig, open up or I won't come to sign the deed." Eager to partake of the American's supposed largesse, Ermanno became irately determined to intimidate another $300 out of me. His bellowing only furthered my resolve not to pay him, and I chose to sit it out. Two hours later he finally left, and I went up to the Socialist bar to have my cappuccino and tell my unreal tale. As Ermanno is a member of the much-scorned rival party, the story was greatly appreciated and commented upon. Of course he would do such a thing, I was told; Communists only know how to rob, cheat, and steal.

Ermanno returned as I was cooking some pasta for lunch. From outside he smelled the frying garlic and hit the door so hard that I expected the lock to break. Again I said nothing, but when the pot of water started to boil and the lid rattled, he lost all rationality, screamed some typical and graphic Tuscan epithets about Mary, whorish and eviscerated, deified dogs and toads, and ended by suggesting that I perform an unnatural act. As I had a meeting in the next town before the signing of the deed in the afternoon, I decided to leave by the front door, which, because my apartments run horizontally through three different buildings, actually exits to another part of the town. As I reached for the front door handle, the pounding suddenly began there. The American-crazed septuagenarian had run the steeply sloped few hundred yards, down and then up, to spring his surprise. I turned around and walked out the other door.

I arrived at the notary by a back entrance, but the wide-eyed secretary informed me, as I suspected, that Ermanno was waiting for me downstairs by the main entrance and would not come up until I spoke with him. Down I went, and we stepped outside. He demanded the money, and I refused. This prompted another tirade, but subdued because of our Main Street location. As I was visibly unimpressed, he suddenly started to tap me on the chest with his forefinger. And so I snapped, summoning up every insulting Italian phrase I could think of, embarrassing Ermanno as windows flew open. Quieted, he agreed to go upstairs, but again only if I would give him the money. I claimed penury, gave him my word, and we signed the deed. I broke my word, and I think I know what he and his friends say about me, but we still are able to sit at a table at the Communist bar and have a glass of wine together.

SORANO 1994

In every country the universal vices and evils of mankind and of human society are considered to be peculiar to that one place. I have never been anywhere where I have not heard people say: "Here women are vain and unpredictable, they read little and are poorly educated; here the people are curious about other people's business, they are lazy and malicious; here money, nepotism, and cowardice are above all; here envy reigns and friendship is false," and so on; as if things were different anywhere else.

PENSIERI 31

With a considered look back at incidents that at the time caused me considerable anguish, like my early attempts at building or the purchase of Ermanno's cantina, I well realize that I was asking for trouble. My funds were limited, and I was trying to buy property and get work done as inexpensively as possible. I could have avoided the unpleasantness with Ermanno by just giving him the little money he wanted. The first time I plastered, I certainly was not knowledgeable enough to know that the pozzolana was of poor quality. I had never plastered before, and I was learning as I did it. It is quite likely that my first effort was unsuccessful because of my bad technique. The two guys I hired to plaster the second time around probably knew as little about plastering as I did. The first builder was immediately available, and he gave me the lowest estimate on the job. I later learned that he had been hired by the town to restore a very important fifteenth-century Medici entrance to the fortress, and the work was done so incompetently that the whole facade collapsed shortly thereafter. Mysteriously, he continues to be in demand, but it can only be because there is so much renovation work going on in the town now.

In time my Italian improved and I became more culturally attuned. I also had the good fortune to work with some discerning and highly trained builders, and I became proficient at every skill involved in building. The first builder, Massimo, helped me with big projects that were not practical to do by myself, like pouring cement floors, and he came up with ingenious solutions to plumbing and electrical problems. I learned an enormous amount just by watching him work. First, his workshop is in immaculate order, all tools clean and in their place. Mine is still a mess, and I do not like to think about the amount of time I have wasted searching for errant measuring tapes and hammers. With the right combination of strength and touch, Massimo can quickly hew a block of yielding tufo or much harder marble to the desired form and size. With the precise hit of a trowel he can break a brick into two equal halves. To observe Massimo the artist/plasterer at work is inspiring. I am envious of his mastery of the single spare movement of expertly scooping an exact amount of plaster from palette to trowel and flicking it onto the wall. Meticulous and fluid, he can plaster in a quarter of the time that I can. Massimo's son Davide has worked with his father for more than ten years, and only recently has Massimo permitted him to begin plastering by himself.

Massimo in his youth was the leader of the Young Communists in Sorano, but later, after the schism between the Socialists and Communists, he dramatically changed his political ideas and is now a member of the Alleanza Nazionale—the Neofascists. Although I have no control over being presumed rich, I have generally followed Leopardi's wise maxim and not let people know about myself or my opinions, political or otherwise. When asked if I support the right or left in the United States, I say that there is not much difference between the two and that I am an Independent. The scandals in Italy of *Tangentopoli* (Bribe City) and the political ascendancies of the media tycoon Silvio Berlusconi, the foul-mouthed secessionist Umberto Bossi, and the Neofascist Gianfranco Fini, I have viewed as remote and bizarre. If I had let on that I am either appalled or offended by this trio who make up the right-wing Polo alliance, Massimo might not have worked with me, and I probably would not be as welcome up at the Socialist bar.

I first encountered Angelo, the other builder I have worked with, when he was renovating an apartment at the edge of the far side of town. I came upon him as he was sifting pozzolana he had collected from a vein he had found down by the river. He was eager to stop and chat, and he had a ready smile that was a bit startling at first sight. As a child he had a fall from his bicycle and lost his two front teeth, which were never replaced. Behind his back he is known as Dracula, but he is a wonderfully friendly and helpful man. He is also very knowledgeable about ancient building techniques and all things Etruscan. We have on a couple occasions gone on walks to fascinating Etruscan, Roman, and Early Christian sites. One time we stopped at a pool in a river. He dove down for a very long time, then came up gasping for air with two fish wriggling in his hands. He caught them by simply grabbing at them after lying in wait at the bottom of an eddy under a rock. This was the Etruscan method of fishing, he proclaimed with his broad curdling smile.

Angelo was happy to work as my assistant for many months, although his experience as a builder was much greater than mine. We plastered and tiled and rebuilt two of my fireplaces, both of which smoked quite badly. Angelo comes from the neighboring town of Pitigliano, and claims that none of the fireplaces there smoke, mostly because they use *enfero*—a very hard form of tufo that reflects heat—to build the base and back. We found a natural deposit of enfero and did as he suggested. We also rebuilt the fireplace hoods, and for whatever reason, the fireplaces now pull beautifully. Although Angelo is economical, he is a slow worker and, when permitted, very long-winded. He also tended to disappear to help an old widow with her leaking roof, or to provide building advice to someone else, or to go down to the river to collect weeds to feed his rabbits, and I often wondered how useful to me he actually was.

As he passed by my open door, Danilo, the last person to have a donkey in town, usually would repeat "*Chi fa da se, fa per tre.*" By doing for yourself, you do the work of three. I am not sure that his saying is true, but I did end up doing most of the work myself. I found that during this time my rhythm and priorities changed completely. I worked for weeks on end, getting up early to labor often until late in the evening. Then, after a few mouthfuls of dinner and a couple glasses of wine, I would collapse in bed. I stopped reading and had no access to any other type of cultural diversions. Before I acquired a modem for my computer, my only sources of news were the television up at the bar in the morning or the Italian newspapers. The only time I went anywhere was to buy building materials or to search in markets for furniture or other objects, such as old porcelain light switches.

I was not thoroughly isolated, of course. I would go up to the piazza every day for an espresso or to do my shopping. I had only to go out either of my doors to find company. At the beginning of the lane, the Via della Sparna, where most of my property lies, Annetta has her home. She is five feet tall, appears to be about fifty, and has the energy of a twenty-year-old. She is in fact seventy-eight, and if she hasn't actually made a pact with the devil, she can certainly be devilishly difficult and mischievous. When I was working on the house, she never failed to stop by when I was having a desperate problem or was thoroughly frustrated and depressed, to tell me in a wickedly baiting way, *"Non capisci niente. Non finisce mai."* You don't understand how to do anything. You will never finish this house. Conversely, she can be very motherly, and I have been to her house countless times for her *acquacotta*, minestrone, polenta, *pasta al ragu*, and chicken or rabbit with roasted potatoes. I have learned many delicious recipes from her. Although some people refer to her as my auntie, often sardonically as she has many detractors, I dubbed her the *Sindaco del Cotone*, the mayor of our part of town. She is insatiably curious about everyone in Sorano and, being quite the control freak, has copies of keys to most of the houses in the old town. Not mine, however, which has been a source of considerable discord.

Almost directly opposite my door on the Via dei Merli is the cantina of "Zio Carlo." Uncle Carlo, as everyone younger than he knows him, makes the best white wine in town. He is about sixty-five and recently retired as the town's plumber. His cantina is a popular destination, mostly for the older set, and in recent years I have found that it is often welcomingly open if I put my head out of my door. If I don't stop by, he will usually yell for me to have a glass before he goes off for an early dinner prepared by his ninety-five-year-old mother, with whom he lives. Carlo's father used the ground floor of the cantina as his smithy when he was one of the three or four blacksmiths that served the town fifty years ago. At harvest time he would roll out his wooden vats and fill them with grapes. After ten days of fermentation, the vats would be drained and the barrels filled with the wine. The barrels were then placed in a room at the bottom of the *gola*, the "throat" of the cantina.

Carlo's cantina has one of the deepest "golas" in town, with steps going down into the tufo some two hundred feet. The room at the bottom, deep in the tufo below Sorano, keeps the wine at a temperature of about 50 degrees Fahrenheit year-round.

Many of the cantinas in town are thought to have been Etruscan tombs before they were found to have an ideal purpose. At one time every family in Sorano had a cantina and made wine in it. Practically every edifice in the old town has a cantina on the ground floor; there are, in fact, more cantinas than the current number of residents. But now there are not more than ten people who continue to use these cantinas to make wine. Most wine is made in more recently constructed cantinas outside the old town, usually directly on the road—making it much easier to bring the grapes there. Every year, I help Carlo harvest his grapes and make his wine, so when I decided to make my own wine, I knew I had been well trained.

Traditional winemaking was a haphazard affair. If the harvest was good, and the sugar content of the grapes high enough, then maybe a passable glass of wine could be produced. Nowadays there are reliable means to prevent excessive mold on the grapes, and if the wine is analyzed, substances can be added to save a harvest that might otherwise produce something mediocre or worse. But there is no way to control the weather, and weather forecasting in Italy in the past was hopeless. Ideally, it will rain towards the end of September, rinsing the grapes, and then not rain again before the grapes are picked, as it is preferable if they are neither wet nor swollen with water. A few years ago, at the time of the harvest, the TV weathermen in their natty Armani suits with epaulets said that the weather would remain good well through the normal harvest period. However, CNN.com was suggesting that a large cold front was coming in, bringing torrential rain, and it would be followed by another—all supported by satellite photographs. Engrossed with my new Internet connection, I chose to heed CNN's warning and decided to harvest early. Everyone thought I was mad when I went up to the bar to say that I was harvesting because of dire warnings on the Internet. "The grapes are not yet ripe, and the sky is clear, but do as you want, Americano," they sniggered. I measured the sugar content of the grapes, determined they were ripe enough, and harvested. The rains arrived soon thereafter and didn't stop for weeks. As a result, mine was one of the few good wines of the year. Some time later, someone saw me in a Harvard Divinity School T-shirt that my father had given me. "Ah, that's why you make such good wine, Americano. You went to a *scuola di vino*. A winemaking school."

The previous year, too, I had arrived back in Sorano just in advance of the grape harvest. I have to be in town at least a week before the harvest if only to take my wooden vats out of the cantina and fill them with water to make the wood expand, closing the gaps where juice would escape when the vats are filled with crushed grapes. I went up under the fortress to Bar Dancing, to buy a newspaper from the ninety-eight-year-old proprietress, Maria, who is far more interested in selling something from her big collection of pornographic magazines than a daily newspaper. She correctly guessed why I was back in town and asked where my vineyard is. I explained that I am essentially a member of a cooperative, because some years I am not around enough to tend to the vineyard myself. I have three long rows of grapes that I pay for by weight when I harvest them. The farmer who cares for the vineyard is named Alfio. "Ah," she said, "Alfio is very ill this year and the grapes are to be harvested by the Cantina Sociale." Maria's information tends to be good, so I was concerned that the big local wine producer might be making off with my grapes.

Later that afternoon in Zio Carlo's cantina I asked the gathered men what the story was on Alfio. One very old man whom I did not know said that Alfio was himself old, and as his two daughters were not willing to take on the running of the vineyard, it and all the grapes had been sold. I thought that Alfio could not be more than fifty-five, so I turned to my friend Domenico, a seventy-five-year-old ex-logger with a huge gut, who also gets his grapes from Alfio. Domenico didn't know how old Alfio was, but he did think he was sick and I had come back too late to reserve my grapes.

The next day, I went to the vineyard and was relieved to find Alfio there, working stripped to his waist and looking fit. With a smile I told him what had been said about him the day before: that he was sick, old, and wanted to sell the vineyard. I thought it was all quite funny. He was livid. "Who told you these lies?" he barked. "With this chest do I look like a man who is sick or old?" He was so upset that he would not even discuss the harvest with me. The next day, I saw Domenico from across the piazza. "O, Americano," he bellowed, "one does not do these things." Alfio, because of what I had told him, had threatened not to give anyone their grapes. Fortunately, he eventually calmed down and we were all able to make our wine.

SORANO 2002

Making wine with Carlo Bizzi

It seems absurd, yet precisely true, that since all reality is nothing, illusions are, in this world, the only true and substantial things.

ZIBALDONE 99

At times there are efforts to deceive, at other times mere exaggeration, or the secondhand telling of a tale causes confusion, misunderstanding, or distrust, particularly in a small town. In Sorano certain people and events tend to alter reality, sometimes to an amusing degree.

The local *casa di riposo* houses the community's aged, infirm, disabled, and insane. Four tittering nuns from India run the institution, as chaste Italian women willing to devote their lives to the Church are apparently in short supply. One or two of the nuns disappear each year, married to local men, but there are plenty more devout Indians ready to take their place. A successful experiment in the 1970s resulted in the town permitting those occupants who are not too incapacitated the freedom to come and go from the home during the day. Some, who may have had violent tendencies, are medicated, and they wander the streets like zombies. Others, like Aldo, are wholly unfettered. He was the first person I encountered when I stepped off the bus on my initial visit to Sorano, and indicated that to get to my destination I should take the road leading out of town. Usually standing at the main intersection of the piazza, Aldo happily continues to give directions to passing motorists. If I see him up to his tricks, I will sometimes intervene. One time he was talking to a middle-aged man in Bermuda shorts. "God, what are you doing in a godforsaken place like this?" the American asked me. "We're just trying to get to Siena." "Are you sure? This nice Italian man just told me to go in the opposite direction." "You're from New York? Jeez, can you believe it, we're from Wisconsin. What a coincidence."

In good weather, Dante, stooped, thin, and silent, will walk in circles, large and small, around the piazza for hours, sometimes followed by a white cat. Other times, townspeople will hand him a leash and he will give their slightly alarmed dogs a long, repetitive walk. If Dante brushes against anything, he will spend a long time desperately trying to wipe away the offending memory with his handkerchief, as he suffers from some sort of cleaning compulsion.

Antonio seems to float as he walks, which is remarkable as he is excruciatingly bent, with one shoulder held much higher than the other. His progress is slow because he pauses between steps, almost elegantly shuffling a foot forward at the last moment, just preventing his large frame from collapsing. Lately, he has occasionally not been moving his feet in time and has confined himself to a stoop. He speaks laboriously and in metaphors. If I see him after a mealtime, I will ask him what he ate. After some seconds he might say, "The stuff you throw at newlyweds."

With his one tooth, sad demeanor, and crumpled hat, Giacomo seemed the most benign occupant of the casa di riposo, but he always managed to unsettle me by raising a finger and warning, "*Non ci passa qui*"—do not pass by here. As I would often meet him at one of the medieval entrances to the town, I fully expected him to intone one day in the words of Dante Alighieri, "*Lasciate ogne speranza, voi ch'entrate.*" Abandon all hope, you who enter here.

According to some people, Graziano was the longest-living person with Down's Syndrome in the world. He was massively obese and enormously patient as the mercurial people in town alternately teased him and stuffed him with pastry and ice cream. During the day he would drift from the Socialist bar on one side of the piazza to the Communist bar on the other. When sitting, he would either idly flip his large handkerchief or accompany himself on a toy accordion, intoning some of the few words he knew. "*Mamma mia. Brutto. La mia.*" Sometimes I would pause and contemplate him, imagining what it would be like to live with no problems, except for the occasional bellyache, and no worries.

Getting directions from a madman is one thing, but when the misinformation comes from a reputable news source, reality can be undermined entirely. During the Gulf War, on January 18, 1991, the newspaper *La Repubblica* reported on its front page that Iraq had fired five missiles on Tel Aviv. At least one of them supposedly had a chemical warhead, and an unspecified number of Israelis had been killed or were suffering in hospital. According to the report, the Israeli government had immediately responded by bombing Iraq. As I happened to be in town, and the only representative of the world's police force, I got into a number of heated discussions. The Communists tended to be most virulent in their attacks against me. Their particular concern was "the American puppet" Israel's bombing of Iraq, as that could have led to a full-scale war in the Middle East. The story was mostly fiction, but as a result of it I got a thorough indication of what a number of townspeople think of Americans. Fortunately, I was not around when the ground phase of the war in Kuwait was initiated.

Another time, I was distractedly watching the news up at the Socialist bar and could only partially hear what the newscaster was saying, because the bar was crowded and I was far from the TV. They were showing pictures of floods in Dakota that I had read about through my Internet provider earlier that morning. Buildings had gone up in flames, and the fires could not be put out because the fire trucks had difficulty getting through the inundated streets, and the water pressure was inadequate. I thought I had misunderstood what the newscaster was saying, because from what I could gather he was claiming that the Americans in Dakota had, in attempting to put out the fires, used so much water that they had ended up flooding the city! Curious, I moved closer to the TV, and my suspicion was confirmed by someone who turned to me with a critical air, proclaiming, "You see, Americano? You people always do things on too big a scale."

Exaggeration worked decidedly in my favor on another occasion. As always, I had left my washed clothes out to dry on a line near my house. I was working with my door open and saw a group of schoolkids, one of whom dropped one of my burning socks. Annoyed, I ran after them, found their teacher, and told her of the incident. As only three of my socks were burned, the loss caused me little worry. Word got around town, however, that the kids had maliciously burned everything on the clothesline, leaving me sockless. The next morning, to my surprise and pleasure, a goodly number of people, some of whom I would never have suspected of harboring the slightest sympathy for the American, presented me with new socks, far outnumbering those with which I had begun.

Generally speaking, the endeavor to seem what we are not spoils everything in the world...And this is true not only of persons, but also of whole societies and peoples. I know several cultivated and flourishing towns that would be very pleasant places to live in but for a distasteful imitation of what is done in the capitals—that is, an attempt to be, in so far as they can, capital cities rather than provincial ones.

PENSIERI 99

One summer I exhibited a room of my home. For ten days in August a few artisans and many merchants set up their wares along a route that passes through the old town. Incongruously, most of the objects came from or seemed to be inspired by far-flung places like Central America, Thailand, and India. On occasional evenings musicians invited by the organizers sang pop songs in English.

At the time, I was completing decorative touches on what is now the living room. Using hand-colored lime, I painted the walls a light pastel yellow, and the fifteenth-century wooden ceiling a light blue. Two thin dark lines mark the change from yellow to blue at the top of the walls, with a broad dark border at the base. Around the perimeter of the room I mounted photographs showing the ruins of homes from the side of town that was condemned and abandoned in the 1950s. Although dilapidated, the interiors showed how houses were traditionally decorated, and the photographs revealed the inspiration for my painted room.

In the early summer, as I was applying one of the ten coats of lime to walls and ceiling, townspeople would stop in to ask why I was not exposing the wooden ceiling and simply whitewashing the walls—a contemporary trend popularized by city "sophisticates" who had been buying up available habitations to use as weekend retreats. It became apparent that the townspeople, some of whom could well remember their old homes, equated the colorful, decorated interiors with what many of them viewed as their provincial and primitive past.

The "far side" of town

To view the exhibition photos in high
resolution color go to www.conigliera.com

During the exhibition, I continued to paint the room and was eager to learn people's impressions of the photographs and the room. I set up a table with glasses and a five-liter bottle of the wine I make in my cantina according to traditional methods. The surprisingly good "American" wine proved to be a successful draw, and the range of thoughts was both amusing and gratifying. One offended sophisticate from Bologna claimed that my painted ceiling was a travesty and, despite my photographic evidence, insisted that I remove the paint and expose the wood. A haughty *professoressa* from Florence congratulated me on my "post-modern" interior design. I was more interested in what the townspeople thought, and most were very complimentary about the room. This was surprising to me, as these new sentiments were in such contrast to almost everyone's initial reservations about the work of period restoration I had proposed. Two elderly men testily asked me why I had gone to all the trouble, but after a glass of wine and a brief discussion, I overheard one remark to the other that being in the room made him feel young again.

The previous owner of my apartment, Ernesto Capelli, quickly recognized the only person pictured in the exhibition. Some time before, I was wandering the empty rubble-strewn streets and noticed that a top floor in one of the abandoned buildings had partially collapsed, revealing a room with what appeared to be a small picture frame and clothes hanging on a peg. I got a painting ladder from my home and balanced it on four blocks of tufo to get up to the bare beams of the second floor, where the boards and tiles had fallen through and been removed. Even more precariously, I then carried up other blocks of tufo, placed them on a beam, and put the ladder on top so that I could pull myself up into the room. As I did so, the ladder slipped and clattered all the way down to the ground floor.

The room seemed perfectly preserved from another time, and I immediately decided to reproduce the pale cyan color of the walls in my own home. There was a single bed, a wooden table and chairs, a small corner closet with some personal items, and a few dresses and shawls on hooks. The brass picture frame contained a photo of an elderly woman. I photographed the room, stepping gingerly as the floor was decidedly unsound and a large crack in the wall indicated that the building was soon to follow others that had fallen into the river valley. I then had to figure out a way to get myself back down. No one would have heard my voice if I were to call for help, so I fashioned a hook out of a hanger, tied the old owner's dresses and shawls together and was able to pull the ladder up, after many tries, from forty feet below. I told the story at one of the bars later in the day, including the detail that I had been tempted to take the lovely frame and picture but had decided to leave it out of respect—and some remorse for having ruined the elderly lady's garments. One week later I walked by the building again and noticed that the frame was gone. Nevertheless, I had the photo, and it was one of the pictures I included in the exhibition. Ernesto said that the woman was his Aunt Teresa Capelli—sister to his father. I learned later in the town hall that Teresa was born on the March 14, 1888, and died on January 21, 1944. Teresa was a spinster and had no children. Ernesto confirmed that I likely was the first person to go into her room since her death forty-five years before.

As I had hoped, several elderly people were moved to stop by during the exhibition and recall how their lives had changed since they had left the old town. Others were able to identify homes and owners from the photographs of the abandoned shells. I have spent a considerable amount of time wandering the streets of the far side of town and could only imagine the vibrant life that would have animated those streets only fifty years ago. On another occasion, I was surprised when a short old woman with white hair and in her black widow's dress appeared at my side. To get to where we were, she must have climbed over a fence and picked her way, somewhat perilously, along a path strewn with broken tiles and blocks of tufo. That had been her home, she explained, pointing up at an open stairway filled with rubble. The black hole in front of us was one of Sorano's four old bakeries. Every week, she went on, her mother would make the dough, stamp it to identify it as their own, and take it to the oven to have it baked, as did the other families. We chatted a little longer, about the relatively poor quality of the bread made by the one baker in town nowadays, and briefly remarked about the lost skills with which every family supported itself in the past, and we went our separate ways.

As I walked away, marveling at how the woman had briefly brought to life the little corner where we were standing, I happily realized how I could get beyond my superficial understanding of the town in which

Teresa Capelli

I live. The quotidian detail about the bakery was already greatly illuminating to me. By relying upon the memories of the old people who had lived in the town, rather than my own romantic imaginings, I could make the town live again, if only in my mind.

I set about interviewing many of the old people I had made contact with in my years in Sorano. I had heard occasional stories and brief histories and legends while I helped Ivana pick her olives, had my morning coffee with Michele, ate lunch with Annetta, or drank wine with Leopoldo in his wine cave, but I now went to them with my tape recorder and asked them to tell me their personal stories and remembrances in detail. Almost everyone obliged me, although some were suspicious of the motivation of the strangely curious American. One would answer volubly, excitedly and tangentially recalling the great history of Sorano, while another would be brief, reluctant to speak about bitter events and the sad "primitive" past. Their collected memories form a broad and eloquent portrait of life in the ancient hilltown. I questioned Luigino, Matilde, and Gino, who had all lived at some time on the short lane where most of my property lies. Peppina and Augusto were born in town, had moved to big cities, but had returned to Sorano and acutely remembered life there before the war.

Maria left Sorano in the 1930s, immigrating to the United States. I found her in an apartment on Webster Avenue in the Bronx. Despite my keen desire to speak again with the old woman in her widow's dress, whom I had encountered alone on the abandoned far side of town, I was never able to find her. None of my old friends knew who she was. I think of her now as my guiding apparition.

...And the old woman sits
Upon the steps with her neighbors
Turning to where the day is dying,
And telling tales how she in better times
Adorned herself on the festival day,
And still healthy and lithe,
Would dance the evening through with those
Who were companions of her lovely prime.

"SATURDAY IN THE VILLAGE" (1829)

> It is curious to observe that almost all men of real
> worth have simple manners; and that almost always
> simple manners are considered of little worth.
>
> PENSIERI 110

That which is beautiful for a person who lives in the city is not necessarily beautiful for someone who lives in a town like Sorano. But, those who live in such a town also want similar comforts like a bathroom, heating, and water in the house. We down here have suffered much for this. I was born on the Via dei Merli—the last house of the town. It is said that it was an old convent. In that house was also born my father who was from 1894. My grandfather inherited the house. My father was born there, my brothers and myself. It was a beautiful house because it had a large kitchen, with an arch, an alcove, a room underneath which you got to by a small stairway, and a little bedroom. However, there was a large fireplace that you stepped up into, and in which you could sit. This house was sold by my brother for 200,000 lire (120 dollars) in 1960. In this house, there was no water because there was water available only from the fountain—that you fetched water from with a pitcher. There was a washroom, but when we had to do our physiological needs, we went into the stable—where there was a *pozzo nero* (black hole.) These stables that we had under the stairs of this house were like a parking garage. There was not the road to go to the town of Sovana (an asphalt road built in the 1930s) and therefore everyone came by way of the old Etruscan paths from all the hamlets of the township of Sorano. Until the late thirties they came by these paths that meet at the road that passes over the river. They came with their *somari* (donkeys.) They brought sheep cheese, eggs, and ricotta to the *bottega*—we called them *lo spaciollo*. In the shop an exchange would be made for salt—they bartered. So they would give and then take these other things in exchange. But they could not go into town with the *somaro*—the female we called *la micia*. So they came with the somaro or with the micia. And they left them in these stalls where the proprietor of this stable tied them up, watched them—and these people paid for this service. These people would come, leave off the donkey, and change their shoes, which were invariably muddy from the journey. Also on Sundays, as not all the hamlets had a church, people would come to Sorano for the mass. And they always came by these roads.

PEPPINA

People came in continuation from all the surrounding hamlets. If you put your face to the window, you would always see a line of people making their way up through the town. That was the station, at Peppina's house, near the Porta dei Merli—the old fortified entrance to the town. Everyone would stop with their donkey. Then in an adjacent cantina, there was a large stone table where the farmers would take their saddlebags full of prosciutto, bread, and cheese. In this tavern, they would have a half-liter of wine and eat. Then they would do their shopping, or go to the collector's office to pay their tribute to the landowners, or up to the town hall to pay their taxes.

ASSUNTA

The best period of Sorano occurred during the 19th century. From the middle of the 18th century through the nineteenth century in terms of the growth of the population, and as regards its economic and social development. During this time they developed all the agriculture, they harnessed the electrical force of the river. They made the die works, two mills, and then in the place of the mills, they set up the power station. This was the development with respect to electricity, and power was produced at Sorano from its two generators to serve many other towns. And then there was further economic development. They established the hospital. They set up a worker's association, by which they constructed the hospital, and founded the *misericordia* as a form of health insurance.

The workers association had the task of helping families in need in the case of sickness. The women would assist another woman who may have been sick and confined to the house. And if a man were sick and couldn't go to the vineyard, the men would go for free and do what was necessary until the sick man recovered. It was a form of insurance.

There was no water, except for the few fountains. Water was at the public fountain. In 1880 they built the aqueduct that brought water from the spring at Vitozza (an abandoned local town at a distance of about eight kilometers). They made a tunnel carved out of the tufo with hand picks from Vitozza to here. It was built well, like a work of art in the real sense. It is only that afterward the pipes were made of terracotta and the new ones that they add nowadays break. Before this time water was collected at the river, or from wells at the fortress. From the roofs, water would be collected, and so they made wells. Otherwise, you would go to the spring with donkeys and barrels. And we from this standpoint were at an advantage because other towns were worse off. At Onano there really was no water. We went down to the river. You washed, you cleaned—there in the river. Until recently from Onano, fifteen kilometers distant, they would come with their clothes to wash them in the river here with donkeys.

MICHELE

Our town was an agricultural town, but always of modest means. Here there were not any large estates, made up of large plots of land. Here one found only little handkerchiefs of land, as our fathers said. Because all the lands were in the control of the Ricci-Busatti family. They had forty-eight farms where they employed farmers as sharecroppers. These sharecroppers had pigs, livestock, and worked like mules to give the owners fifty % of their harvest, and all of their expenses. The owners could permit the luxury of having an administrator who would go to supervise, even if the farmers were taking even just a basket of acorns to give to their pigs.

PEPPINA

From the 1800s, the lords of the town were the families Selvi and Busatti. The Selvi came from Grosseto—they had two rocks (castles) there—and the Busatti were the lords from here—with big balls (powerful). The Ricci came after the Busatti. They established a bank that served, still during the 19th century, as a place to deposit money that they would give to families in need. Sorano was not a rich place because ninety % of the land was in the hands of these two families. The Selvi being from Montorio, (a hamlet 6 kilometers from Sorano). The Soranese had their tiny plots of land just directly around Sorano. It was very little. Just a small plot. Those that worked here, other than the Soranese, were people that came from around Pistoia. They came here to work the land for the wealthy families. They ate and slept in an inn, adjacent to where I now live called the Three Stars of David. Jews ran it. There was a significant Jewish community here. Here there is the Ghetto quarter, which was where the Jews lived.

So, before there were the Busatti, then came the Ricci. Then there were the Cavallini, but they are all of the same family. The palazzo and the fortress were theirs. They had practically all the lands, the farms and farmhouses, and the large farmhouses between here and Pitigliano (eight kilometers distant). The houses—the little rooms—were owned by the people. We did not live well because the lords of the town, the Ricci/ Busatti and Selvi were the owners of almost all of the territory. The rest of the people were tenant farmers. Half of the produce went to the owners. If it was eggs, maize, grapes, olive oil—it was all divided in half. The rich took advantage of the poor. Even speaking of the smallest parcels of land, those who were privileged owned most. Of 400 families, fifty were landowners of some type—this was the sphere of small owners. Then there were the big landowners—this was the nineteenth century up until 1945 when they instituted the agrarian reforms of *L'Ente Maremma*[3]

Michele

---

[3] Before World War II, Tuscany was still essentially a feudal society. In the 1950s, the Maremma Authority was established by the Italian government to redistribute 100,000 hectares of land from wealthy landowners to the rural peasantry.

Because Sorano was a town in the middle of Italy—not having a rail station nearby, not having industries—it was never developed. All the people that lived in Sorano did with what little that was reaped from the earth. And that earth is very dry and very poor. That earth always gave few fruits in comparison to what was required by the family. But the families, even if they were not well off could live because they had the wheat, which they harvested, corn, which they picked, potatoes, and fruit. Each year the family killed a pig, which one would buy every year on the sixth of January when there was the market. That is when you would buy a little piglet; you would fatten it throughout the year and in December kill it. The meat was salted and it would keep for the full year. First came the sausages, then *capocollo, prosciutto, salame* etc. With it, we might have *polenta*.

PEPPINA

My father worked for himself, but also for others. He had land, but it was far away. It took two hours to get there, by foot. When the water was high at the channel—there is a ravine on the way up—you would have to go a long way around. When it rained, and the ravine was full, you couldn't pass by the road, and you would have to go by a longer and more difficult way, following old paths. We would pass through the land of the Cavallini family, but if the water in the creek were high, we would have to go by the old paths and pass by the long way. La Rotta, San Tomaso (local small hamlets) and then Sorano. We had land at Sambuco, and then a piece at Prati—land *we* had. Also from my mother's side. And then there was the vineyard at Pian di Sotto. So we harvested enough. We would go there with the donkeys. When we went to pick, we went by foot. At this point, all the land has been sold, except for that at Pian di Sotto, which went up in fire last year. We made good wine from there. And we sold it. How else would you pay the taxes or have shoes made?

MARIETTA

This was survival. So the people who were relatively well off—those few that you could count with one hand, who were employed by the local government—they had a fixed stipend. But the farmer worked the year round, and if the eternal father was indulgent and did not send down hailstones when the grapes were harvested then a goodly amount of wine was made, and so a barrel of wine was sold. With that barrel of wine that was sold one could by shoes for the children, one could buy an overcoat—that was it.

PEPPINA

My grandfather had a wine press. Not everyone had a wine press back then. He had a press that many used. It was much bigger, and he made it because he was a wood worker. It had a big screw made out of wood, and a large wooden handle that required two men to turn it. At one time he would sell the remains of pressed grapes to Siena, where they would make grappa. The remains in my time cost money. Now they throw them away.

MATILDE

There were 4000 poor people here. There wasn't enough for clothes, shoes or food. There was nothing. There were very few who were "rich"—who could eat meat with their bread. I was somewhat better off than most because my poor father had two hectares of land. So with two hectares of land you were a "lord," *allora*. Because you could provide wheat, maize and olive oil for the house you were a lord.

MICHELE

Previously everyone worked, because before they worked the land. So there were the few rich, and we poor—and the life was like that, not like it is now when everyone is dressed well. If you came to the houses, it was *minestra* all the same. These were poor towns. You kept yourself going with the work in the countryside.

MARIETTA

We were always hungry because there was no substance to what we ate. In the morning when my father got up to feed the donkey down at our stall, he would say, "Hey get up and put the pot on for the polenta." And what did you eat it with? You would fry up an onion. By the time we ate our bean or bread and onion soup in the evening, we were dying of hunger, and then it never was really satisfied. We ate even in the middle of the night—a nut or a slice of apple. Our house was one room, with three beds placed side by side. We were two big girls in one single bed. One pulls the covers here, the other there. She took more room, I less. I was nineteen, and she was sixteen. We argued for space in the bed, and she knocked me over the head with a cup. I got married that week with a black eye.

ASSUNTA

Here there was the lord and the vassal—the vassal had the land but was a sharecropper. At the end of the year, half of the crop had to be given to the landholder. The poor had a "handkerchief" of land. We, most of us lived under modest circumstances, because Sorano was not developed in any way. There wasn't craftsmanship—there was no industry of any type. The only craftsmen we had were down at the pottery, on which a rather numerous family lived well. There were other artisans, but not of the type that lends to development. There were the local artisans like the cobbler to resole shoes, the barber who shaved the townspeople, and

Michele *in 1963 was backed by the Communists to become mayor of Sorano. Now in his late seventies, he spends much of his days at the bar that serves right leaning patrons. He rarely misses early afternoon TV viewings, with Nadia the proprietress, of "The Bold and the Beautiful," the American soap opera that is known as "Beautiful" in Italy. Otherwise, he plays cards, or holds court. Being of an independent mind, he usually remains above the fray. Unlike those screaming about him, he tends to speak in broader strokes, politically and historically. During one of our discussions about wartime Italy, a hardened Communist interrupted to detail his personal injuries at the hands of the Fascists and Christian-Democrats. Michele's dismissive riposte was that Communism had failed and only caused suffering to vast populations. Michele is also exceedingly helpful in resolving bureaucratic problems or explaining arcane tax details, so he is much sought after. When I was finally able to get him to agree to a taped interview, it was only as a quid pro quo, however. It was the time of the vendemmia, and he needed me to help empty his tubs full of harvested grapes into the large vat in his cantina. We agreed to meet at the bar and then walk down to the cantina in the center of town. Much to Michele's delight, I brought along Pia a blonde, tall, statuesque and tattooed Swedish girlfriend of mine, who was there helping me with my own winemaking. Dressed in a tight black pair of jeans and skimpy t-shirt, she caused quite a stir on that particular afternoon. We were joined by several other titillated older men who, for the occasion, were brought together regardless of political persuasion. Once the work was done, we sat and drank Michele's sweet white wine, of which he is duly proud. Michele was concerned that glasses remained full, particularly Pia's, and his thoughts ranged from making out with girls at the water fountain (where everyone got their water for use at home), to illegitimate children (of which there were many who were deposited at the church steps in baskets called bastardi—thus the origination of the word bastard) and exotic actresses (speaking of the '30s Russian/ Italian film star Assia Norris—who Pia reminded him of—he digressed into a somewhat convoluted tale of the cinema, Italy's pre-war imperialism, and Fascism.)*

Michele Savelli

the joiner who made repairs or made closets. They lived by their trade, but these were not artisans, that employed ten, or five boys to learn the trade. Of builders, there was one family—the father of Tetta, and his sons. It was a little family business. They were all trained in the arts of the builder. The people who were a bit more skilled would learn, and then be able to work. They were capable of putting together four blocks or fixing broken steps. But there was not this culture of the house. Already just to paint the house was costly—it represented luxury.

PEPPINA

After the 1800s, from 1915 or 20 began the decline of Sorano. From 4000 inhabitants, the population began to fall. They fell in intelligence and activity. That which was constructed was done by past generations, and we, even the best of us, have done nothing more. What there was, they have even destroyed. The bank—they destroyed. The mills—destroyed. The electrical system—destroyed. The workers association—destroyed. The hospital—closed. The fascist period was the period of the decline, from 1915-1940. As regards population, if you also count the hamlets of Catabbio and San Martino there were 9,000 inhabitants in the township of Sorano, but the population of the main town of the district was 4,000. The Busatti family did good, but it also did bad. For example, that big palace that they constructed at the beginning of this century up by the fortress—to build it they destroyed the ancient walls of the town, and the bastion that existed there. Before the Busatti *palazzo* was where the pharmacist is now.

MICHELE

The owner that we knew was a Ricci. Her husband died, but they had children. The one child who married Cavallini was the owner of everything, and he ate all the money by gambling—he lost every-thing—all he was left with was a farm that they no longer own. Some Sardinians bought the villa and farm. So, of them, we know nothing more.

Leopoldo

And then we kept corn, grain, and meat. It was all hung in the house. We were surrounded by the stuff because most people back then did not have storage areas as they were already filled with families. Yes, there were rats, fleas, flies—a bit of everything—but we were well off because we were many.

Marietta

All in that one room there were: the *povera* Ciuccia with her husband, and the mother of Noverra with her husband, divided from them by a curtain. Then there were the parents-in-law. Then just inside the door, there was the fireplace and some sacks of wheat. And there was maize all hanging around the beds. Two families surrounded by sacks of wheat and maize. The mother in law with the daughter in law, who was mar-ried and with a son. The son was known as *Cenciapane* because when we are young, we all have difficulty speaking in on way or another. He should have said "*senza pane,*" but he would say "*cencia pane, cencia caccio a scuola non voglio anda.*" Without bread, without cheese, to school, I am not going. His father when he came home from work would say "*so cotti?*" Is it cooked? (Is dinner ready?) He was known as *Socotti.* Everyone had nicknames like these. Anyway, there were seven or eight people, a pig, the grain, the maize, the washtub, and the wood—all in a room of about 300 square feet.

Matilde

My poor father was good—he married three times. His first wife produced three children, us two and one that died. His third gave birth to two more. And the six of us were well off as compared to most. But, it was a very poor town. The families of those that were employed, or that lived in the Ghetto lived well enough. He who had a pension from having fought during the war of 1915-18 was a big lord because he got 100 lire a month. This was not a big or rich town; it was a town that suffered its share. Eighty % lived in two or only one room. All inside. There was a room and the kitchen, with a curtain that divided the space. Or you could find the bedroom, the kitchen, the stable with the donkey and pig—everything. You understand how they lived? There were four thousand in this small place. Where do you put them all? They lived inside of caves. Many of the houses were cut out of the rock. There they would make the bedroom, another room, and then at night they would dig away some more and make another hole to put another child inside.

MICHELE

Half of the home that I lived in after I was married was built into the rock. We used the grotto for storage, for wood and rounds of cheese. There was a door, but the walls of the grotto were part of the home. When it rained, so much wetness came into the house that I had to make a hole in the floor, which passed into a stable below, to stop the kitchen and beds from being flooded.

ASSUNTA

The only thing for those who were somewhat better off was to have an ass that carried wood or wheat—also you did the wine harvest always with the donkey. The donkey demonstrated the wealth of the house. A house where one was well off was a house that was always still modest. Then there was the donkey. Then there was the pig that was bought. The pig, chickens, and donkey were kept in the stable. There were very few who kept the animals in the house with them, but they existed. At my house, my mother was very clean, even if the house was with rustic tiles. We would make up the table always with a white tablecloth. We had these animals that toiled for us and provided us with food. So we did not suffer because we had everything in the house. We had bread, we had prosciutto, we had eggs, we had chickens, we had fruit—we had everything. We did not lack for anything. The men worked very hard however.

PEPPINA

There were important seasonal events. The *mettitura*—in June, when the wheat is planted. The *trebbiatura*—when the wheat is harvested. The *vendemmia*—wine harvest. The picking of the olives. They did the pressing cold back then, with big round crushing stones. There were parties associated with particularly the vendemmia. Every family made wine. The days of the harvests were long. To walk to Sull'Oro, one of the best places to grow grapes and where Leopoldo and my uncle had their vineyards, took half an hour. To bring back the grapes you would need eight to ten voyages with the donkey that could carry two wooden *bigonsi* with 220 kilos of grapes, one on either side. Along paths and dirt roads, down to the main piazza, which was not even paved until the mid-60s. Nowadays you do one voyage with a tractor. At the end of the day, everyone would gather in the cantina for a meal, and to press the grapes. Then for the *svinatura* two weeks later, when you drain the vats of the new wine, there was a big party with salted cod and onion. Everyone was on the streets and in the cantinas.

ALBERTO

No one had money. You had a piece of earth in which you could plant potatoes for the need of the house. Let's say that there were 200 kilos left over—but to sell these extra potatoes, to whom you would you give them? Either you gave them to those who had none—but we had to sell them. There were no trucks, so we traveled in carts, with donkeys or with horses, etcetera. Someone came from outside looking for potatoes. So, who arrived first sold his potatoes—all the others were left with no recourse. It was a life like this: try to scrape by. In my house, I had a grandfather. In fact, he was an uncle of my mother, who adopted the children of my mother—he had no children of his own. His brother, however, had a mountain of children. My mother was the last—either the seventh or eighth child—so he adopted my mother. My uncle/ grandfather had the fortune of being the town's dustman. At the end of the month, he took home his wages. Very few people received wages: those that worked in the town's administration, and the dustman. He was also the gravedigger—he put everyone under from the whole township. He was the gravedigger, undertaker, and dustman. Sorano at the time was an even bigger township, and my "grandfather" did this type of work—he had to go and bury the dead in these distant hamlets. He had such a big heart although he never went to church. When he returned home from work, he would mend the shoes for those that were without—he would re-sew them. Otherwise, they would go barefoot. I would not joke about this. There was terrible poverty here.

LEOPOLDO

What did my husband do? He lived with the donkeys, more than anything (laughs.) He was a farmer. His father had three other donkeys. And then he had hangovers. But he also worked at the tufo quarry, cutting blocks. He died because of that work. He died at fifty-one. He began working there in '69. By 1973 he was dead, after only five years. They're dead all of them. Moscino, Tonino. They are all dead of heart attacks, of straining, and then they all drank. The truck drivers would bring them up the wine. They earned little, drank a lot, and ate little. One falls—and the work was very tiring. Poor things.

MATILDE

We made our own bread. You heated the water and made the bread. When it rose, you took it down to the baker. Every eight days—but for the big families, it was not enough. If you didn't have bread, you went and looked for some from another woman. Instead, my father did not want to give out bread. He thought why didn't they calculate better? If they needed bread a day sooner, why didn't they make their bread a day earlier? There was my poor grandmother—the mother of my father. She was very precise so that she would clean the grain by hand—and she wanted her own flour when she went to the mill. But she also did not want to give her bread to anyone else. Because she would say that everyone must eat their own bread. You know who was really *sciorno*? You remember poor Mario—his poor mother was always going around asking for money and bread. And you have to think that room you bought was full of grain because they had a threshing machine. And they sold the grain. But there were many children. We, however, never went around asking anything from anybody.

MARIETTA

There wasn't enough bread. There was not enough wheat for the needs of the family. So they survived with maize and potatoes. They ate more than anything *polenta* (maize meal pudding) because it was easier to get maize than wheat. The families that had a sufficient amount of wheat were few. For meat, they raised rabbits, hens, and pigs. So they would kill them, and would survive the winter with the meat of a pig. The pig they would kill and hang in the room, attached to the beams. Then there would be the flies when the meat went bad.

They worked to eat because that which they planted or raised they ate. I mean to say, before there was a butcher, and they could not make ends meet. Now the butchers are slaughtering from morning to night.

In the houses, there were few toilets. They would make a hole and then clean the hole out occasionally—the *pozzo nero*. The flies were frightening because, in the stables of the donkeys—and here there were many donkeys—the stable during winter is warm, and the flies do not die. When spring arrived, they came out, and they were all there. In the back of my grandfather's stable was a pozzo, deep 2.5 meters by 1.2 meters. My grandfather would put the waste in there. When it was winter, and the *stabbio* was ripe, he would tell me to take the pitchfork and go inside the *pozzo*. So I went in with the pitchfork and cleaned out all of the compost. The flies were big like this. They went in my mouth, all over. It was an organic fertilizer that was taken into the countryside with donkeys. Otherwise, when they cleaned out the holes, it was taken away directly and put in caves or other places. The waste from the house was thrown out the windows, however.

MICHELE

Here it was cold, but bearable in the house because with the donkeys we would bring large logs, and the fire was kept going in the fireplace. It would be started up in the morning and kept burning till night. The fireplace was used for preparing meals in the summer too.

MARIETTA

In the evenings, as I lived up at the Poggio fifty years ago, there was no gas. Nothing. All was done with the light of the fire. And there was so much smoke that got into your eyes. There was also coal, but in the evening you would go around looking for wood to light it with—the smoke was at eye level. In front of the fire, you'd burn yourself—on your back you would freeze. We would put up a little curtain just below the mantle of the fireplace to try and stop the smoke. You just have to imagine, above you'd be choking on smoke, below you would be burning, and in the back freezing. Behind was the kitchen with a pitcher of water, and that pitcher would be frozen solid. In the house, if you would put out a sheet to dry, in the morning it was frozen. You know back then how cold it was up at the Poggio? Now it no longer snows. But back then the snow came in the house. It would come in from the roof. I had it in bed, and the snow would come up high like this. I was under with the snow on top. There was a pyramid of snow above us *guancialone* (pillows.) It was so cold. It seemed like something unthinkable.

MATILDE

During winter the family was all together, gathered around the fire. Mothers worked with wool. They made socks; they spun the wool to make the socks. On Sundays, the family would play bingo. During the summer there were the townspeople who had gone to the city, and returned—thus there was a little more activity, a few more parties. You could also go and buy an ice cream, that cost six soldi. Half a *lire* for the ice cream, and four *soldi* for the cone. Every year, the first Sunday of May, the children put on their best clothes and went to Mass in new shoes. The first week of June there were the communions. There were some wonderful meals. These were the amusements. In August there were other festivals. We ate a lot of sweets. But most everything revolved around nature. According to what was harvested. Because they saw very little money. Now I am speaking of a time that was reasonably thriving.

PEPPINA

We would wind up the wool on the spindle. You want to see mine? I still have it. With spit, you used to wind the wool thread. Before you did not just sit around doing nothing. Or instead of spit, you'd bathe your hands in water. Or you'd get the dry chestnuts. You would put the dry chestnuts in your mouth, and that would make you slobber all over. During the time of the war, everyone was spinning wool, to make socks. They used to say when the spindle fell there was no longer the desire to work. Because they were so tired.

MATILDE

Peppina *and I met at my adoptive "aunt" Annetta's apartment for the second installment of her deliberative social history of Sorano. She was still flush from a heated argu-*  *ment she had with Lori, a schoolteacher and niece of the president of the local party of the Right (formerly Socialist and now Forza Italia.) Lori had criticized the Communist mayor, suggesting that he must be even more corrupt than the previous Socialist mayor. Peppina, a bred in the bone Communist, and perhaps emboldened by the recent formation of Italy's first Leftist government, gave Lori a highly principled tongue-lashing. Annarella, blissfully ignorant of politics, sat with us at Annetta's table. She had witnessed the venomous confrontation that morning and was quite upset that the two ladies could have struck at each other with such rancor. Annoyed, Peppina continued her diatribe. Political ideas are essential, she said. They indicate the ideology of a person, and that ideology dictates how that person thinks and lives. The underlying hypocrisy of Lori's political stance, and that of practically everyone from Sorano who supports the Right is that it is a total repudiation of their humble, yet noble, origins. Ninety-five % of the townspeople are the sons and daughters of tenant farmers. Forty years before, as much because of their lack of education as their common heritage, the townspeople were united as a family. Nowadays people are so divided by politics that they do not respect one another's ideas and cannot even treat one another with civility. At seventy Peppina is the youngest townsperson that I have interviewed, but her memories, particularly of the difficult war years and the considerable changes that occurred thereafter are vivid. Hers was the first generation to benefit from Mussolini's reforms in education, but, as she would say, this did not come without the insidious effects of indoctrination. She did, however, receive more schooling than the older women with whom I have spoken. Peppina went on to Rome where she lived, continued her education and married, and had returned to Sorano only in recent years.*

You would start with a big roll of wool, and then very slowly with the spindle, you would make the yarn so that you would have all the spindles full and then you would make the balls of yarn. You would have to put your fingers in your mouth so that the wool would slide better. You boil the skins of the walnut, which you remove when they are green, which makes the water dark brown. And you put the socks in the hot water, and they became brown. And it would not come away. If you rub those green skins on your hands, they remain brown. To make white, you would use sulfur. This was also an old technique. With the sulfur vapors you would make pieces of stitching white.

ASSUNTA

We would dry the fruits—plums, peaches, and figs—above a baker's oven in the *graticcio,* a basket made from old man's beard—a wild vine that climbs up into the trees. You put the wheat in the *pagliccia,* made from straw,. Then there were the *paniere*—baskets all of them made by hand. And then there was her father who made with straw the baskets specially designed to spread wheat seed. In the buckets, or in the larger baskets, the seed escaped, so with these little ones, made with very fine straw, they would make them the size of a quart or a pint. This sort of thing I did myself. The hemp was used for making sheets and clothes and linen for the kitchen. I seeded it during the war in the garden near the one of Michele. There were the hemp growers of the river, who called themselves *Canapai*—I did precisely this work during the war. The hemp was seeded, and in August the plants were cut. They were high like this, white, not like the yellow color of more mature plants. Then they were tied together in bunches and left to soak in the river. Or they were left in hot water—at the *Bagno di Santa Maria.* The *Bagno* was a lovely hot spring we all remember. But it dried up because the vein of hot water was interrupted when they created the tufo quarry. Afterwards, the hemp bunches were untied, and beaten with a piece of wood. The husks were removed and you were left with strings of hemp like cotton. After that, the strings of hemp were left to dry in the sun—on top of the pottery. Then they were wound into balls and used on the handlooms to make sheets. There was a room full of looms down under the house of Maya, where the women worked. After the sheets were made, they were taken down to the river. There they were washed in the water—*curare il pano*—then hung out to dry in the sun, rewashed, and then re-hung until it became white. Before, there was no bleach.

MATILDE

They had to take the dirty laundry, put it in a basket, and take it on their heads to a washhouse in summer and winter—even when it was freezing out. Then the washing was put in the *conca*—the wash tub—still somewhat soapy from the rinsing at the washhouse. Then the laundry was covered with a cloth. Then one would take a *paiolo* (a cauldron made of copper) in which you would boil water at the fireplace. You would take some of the cinders from the fireplace, placing them on top of the cloth. Then you would pour the cauldron of boiling water over it all, which would whiten the wash, and from this *conca*, in which there was put a small tap at the bottom, the boiling water would flow out, still hot with the filtered ash—like you would make coffee—and out would come this water which we called il *ranno*—lye. Nowadays we use bleach. Afterwards, in this ranno we would put the colored wash. After the laundry was taken out of the ranno it had to be carried down to the river, and the women bent over, with their knees on a rock, and on another rock the laundry was beaten, then rinsed, and then hung over the lawn by the river. After they had dried, they were collected, and they had the lovely smell of the ashes—of fresh laundry really.

PEPPINA

In the conca you would put the laundry, then boiling pots of water, and above it all ashes from the fire. And it would come clean—perfumed.

Then the laundry was taken down to the river to be rinsed, on our knees, mothers, and daughters down on the rocks by the River. We would carry down the wet hemp sheets that weighed a lot—one trip for the sheets alone. Now they have sheets made out of pure silk.

MATILDE

This morning I did not get up until 8:30. When I had to work for the family—I would get up very early in the morning. Also, I worked as washer maid here. There was no water—I would take it to the *signore*. There was no water—there were not even toilets. We would wash our clothes at the river's edge. And they would become perfumed, you know. Down there the water was clean, and you could rinse as many times as you wanted. Nowadays with the washing machines they rinse, but it isn't the same thing. But I must say that I am happy that at least I have this (pointing to the washing machine). How could I go down to the river now? Like now, there are all of these conveniences. Listen—one day you would have to go to the washing house to soap up the clothes. The next day you would have to get wood to boil the clothes, put them in the *conca*—Annetta still has one—and the next day you would have to go down to the river to rinse them. But my life has not changed so much by and large. I don't have a flushing toilet. I don't have hot water.

MARIETTA

We'd also go down to the river to clean—to rub in the sand the spoons and forks. And then for Easter, they took all the copper things from the house. They went down to the river, cleaned them all in the sand, and then rinsed them in the water. And then they were all set out to dry on the grass. This was done once a year. All the pots and pans—the beautiful baking tins of copper. Then when there was the war and they all went to the war effort—everything for the war. Bed pans, the big amphorae for water, which you carried on your head—so they carried them all down to shine them at the river.

MATILDE

Near Easter we went with all of the jugs made of copper—the casseroles, the pans—down to the river and with the sand we cleaned and polished all these objects and then took them back up to the house, and left them out for everyone to admire. Because also at Easter, as spring was arriving we would clean also the whole house, we would change those curtains that divided the house, because the parish priest would come by to bless the houses.

The situation for women was very unsatisfactory. The woman had to be wife, mother, housewife, farmer, and laundress—she did everything. They made their own bread, for instance. Only once a week, but they made ten loaves. They were put in a *panaio* made of wood and lined with white cloth, and each loaf was placed in there divided from each other. At 5 in the morning, the baker would call *"Fa Pane, Fa Pane"*. They would add the yeast. When it had risen, it would be taken to the oven. The baker would put it in, and when it was cooked, you would go to collect the bread. This bread would last for eight days. I speak of the women. The men would go to the mill to grind the flour. The women had the work of washing and making the bread. And then they had the responsibility to help the men in the fields, with some of the slightly less arduous work. The men who were a little more "violent"—and we must speak of violence—would take their women also to dig and to hoe. Whereas those who were a little more civil would take their women to do the tying up of the grape vines, to choose the wheat, or dig up potatoes. But this is all to say that the women were sacrificed. They were very tired.

PEPPINA

Do you want to know about my life? I always worked—I worked the earth. My husband was shot in the neck in a hunting accident. It happened with Sarino when I was thirty-eight. He remained speechless and paralyzed. He could not work. My only son—he died twenty-one years ago. There was a landslide that fell on his back in a cantina. He was thirty-six years old. So we went on without money. In the beginning, I was always at the house because I had to give my husband massages, to help him walk, eventually. When I was in Rome, I went to the house of a cousin. One day there came someone who did these massages—a nurse. And I said, I don't have money to pay for this, and so I decided to learn how to do these massages. And so when they released him from the hospital in Rome they told me he was paralyzed and they could no longer keep him. So I learned how to do these massages, and so, in the end, he walked a little bit, but his foot he dragged, and the arm remained useless. And I got on with tending the land. And then we had to put up with the war. And these mothers scarcely had bread—what do you think? There also came the son of Castrini. His mother would say to me, take my son with you to help you work and just give him bread because I don't have any—because I had some—understand? And so like this, I cared also for the vineyard, with the help of some men. Sometimes they would come and help me. Sarino died in 1980. My son—in 1974. Yes, he would help too, but he died immediately, for pity's sake.

MARIETTA

On Sunday the men would change themselves and then go to the *osteria*, to play cards and drink. Then they would return home, and weigh on their wives. They would go to bed with their wives. There were no contraceptives, and they would have six, seven, eight children... It is not as if they wanted all these children... they came.

PEPPINA

My mother... when a mother has eight children and is able to maintain so well the hearth... My mother was on top of things, for the love of God. My brother Lorenzo, the first son, was from 1908. My mother beat him before he chose his wife because she didn't joke. When you want sons, it is necessary to produce them. She would give him a smack on the back. In all, she had sixteen children. Some died in childbirth, others were miscarriages, etcetera. She would go out to work with a child hanging around her neck, and another by the hand.

LEOPOLDO

In the past, there were more sicknesses. More died when they were small, or when they were born. Of my family, two died when they were small. So whoever had the fortune to grow was tested. Those that died, and there were many, were called *Morticelli*. They would take away these dead in the little boxes made with strips of wood in which they would sell soap. My poor grandfather was a joiner, and he made these little coffins with the strips of wood from the soapboxes—to spend little. Two soapboxes, a touch of paint, and then children would take the coffin up to the cemetery on their shoulders. They'd be paid a lira each. My brother died at five months, to carry him up to the cemetery he was put in one of these little boxes. And they carried him up, four little boys, in a little cart. I was twelve when that happened. More than sixty years ago. Now it doesn't seem real or possible. But you saw this every day. And to carry my little brother up each boy was paid a lira. The priest gave him a little splash of water, and away he went. The dustman would take it up under his arm—the uncle of Leopoldo. But it was not necessary to take these children to the church—they were little angels. It's not as though they had sinned.

ASSUNTA

Then there was rickets, the period of tuberculosis and malaria. When the men had to go and work in the low lands of the Maremma they had to use quinine as a measure of prevention against malaria. Even here at school, they gave us preventative doses of quinine in school. They would give us little squares of chocolate with the quinine inside. It was a little bitter, but we took it because it was an important prevention. This they did this during the fascist times from 1922. But here there were only a few who died of malaria—more from tuberculosis.

There was a nursery school for children—a communal school. In Sorano, there was never a middle school up until 1947-48. After the war the priest, if you went to him, helped as a tutor—or the boys who wanted to study went to the seminary. Even if they did not have a job, they would pretend that they wanted to be priests, and then after they had finished schooling, they would leave. Meanwhile, the girls would go to work the fields or sew... The children of the farmers got to fifth grade at best. At age ten or eleven you were finished with school. Those that continued with school were only the son of the doctor, the son of the pharmacist, or the daughter of the town hall secretary that took advantage of a scholarship that we did not know existed. Which, instead of being granted to those who merited it—those who may have been poor, or who may not have the fascist membership card—it was given to the lords or to someone who worked for the town hall, who happened to already have a fixed income, which may not have been great, but at least he was well off because he was assured to have bread. Whereas the men working in the fields never were assured of having bread. They would go to the only middle school that was nearby which was ten kilometers away, only until age fourteen. From Sorano to Pitigliano there was no public transport, so already it was practically impossible—or to pay the fees—so nobody went. It was not really that there was not the intellectual possibility. It was that there was not the economic possibility. This was a great deficiency. Because as we in Sorano were relatively few, there were those who were intelligent, who could do things—study—who could have a certain position in society—even be useful to society—and yet this was practically not possible. The sons of the farmers already at fifteen were working in the fields, and when June came around—the middle of June—they would leave to go work down in the Maremma, to earn a little money. They went to scythe the wheat. Then they did the sifting of the grain. Then they harvested the straw. They slept in the stables, or under the trees. This was the life of the farmers—of the work that they did. In fact the story of Italy wherever it may have been—In Abruzzo, Lazio—the life in the countryside in sum.

PEPPINA

Listen to what our old men did when they went down to the Maremma. After they had walked two or three days, with that terrible heat. They made the *panzanella*. Bread was left to soak in a big tub of water. They would add a drop of olive oil, and after working twenty hours with that sun that killed you, that was dinner. My poor husband, when he was my fiancé and was eighteen years old, he sent me a postcard from down there. He wrote me with a matchstick that he would light and then blow out. It seemed like a piece of charcoal. I am speaking of fifty years ago.

MATILDE

The main drag, *la Passeggiata,* was from this door here, which is where there was a joiner. *Da Capo*—the "beginning" at Piazza Manfredo Vanni where you are now, up to the *Alberi* (trees) in the piazza. *Da Capo agli Alberi.* Then you would return back down again because the women were all down here. From the Piazza del Municipio (the main town square) on up, there was no one. And there was a custom: the fathers would not let the women walk around because they should not just go around. The fathers were jealous of their girls, and they did not want that they talk with the young men. So, they went to the fountain to collect water with a pitcher. They would throw out the water to have the excuse to go to the fountain. There they would find girls that they would make out with on the street.

MICHELE

Before I was very pretty, now I am *bussolotta*. So, one night Avio, my husband to be, asked me to go dancing. But, alone you could not go—we had to be accompanied. When it was eight in the evening, everyone had to be at home. I was eighteen or so and weighed maybe one hundred pounds. I had put on a lovely dress, and I don't know where I had found it, but I had put just a touch of pink on my lips. My father as I was going out the door noticed. He said, "where do you think you are going with that mask on your face. You are going straight to bed." I soaked my pillow with tears that night.

So, Avio was a relation of Mario who had a house opposite a fountain. We used to make love. When Avio wanted to see me—we would hardly ever see each other, and never in the evenings—he would sit in the window waiting for me to come to the fountain to get water. So, I would go—I was only fourteen and very foolish—with the pitcher to get water. We would go down into one of the cantinas. When I got home, my mother would ask what took so long, as she was waiting to prepare the evening meal. I would say, Mamma there was a long line, I had to wait my turn. Of course, it wasn't true.

IVANA

There were many people on the streets. There were the joiners, the cobblers, the blacksmiths—these types. There were seven cobblers, who would make new shoes, but also repair the old. In the Piazza Manfredo Vanni, there were two. Then there were some down at the Borgo—two or three. There were four barbers. Women worked as the bakers. One woman alone would prepare the oven, and then every family would bring its own bread to have it cooked. It is not as though they made bread, as the baker does nowadays. There were four or five ovens for baking. In different parts of the town—the Borgo, the Poggio, down at Cotone, at the Ghetto. They were lit at four in the morning. The women in their homes prepared the bread, and when the oven was ready, the people would bring their bread to have it cooked.

Luigino *was forced to stop working as a potter in the 1950s, because of a sharp decrease in demand for ceramic wares. He became a builder and emigrated from Sorano. After he had retired in the early eighties, he returned to town and again took up his trade. When I first interviewed Luigino, it was shortly after he had suffered a massive heart attack at age seventy-five. His condition, which had*  *made him pale and gaunt, accentuated the barrel chest and large, powerful hands that he had labored with since childhood to collect, prepare and throw clay. I was particularly eager to talk and learn from Luigino as I too throw, and have studied with and photographed other master potters in Europe, the U.S., India, and China. Our conversations were spare as he is by nature taciturn, but also because he was concentrating on throwing the two times I interviewed him—there were silences as he centered the clay on the wheel, pulled up the walls of the vessel and then refined the form. On the first occasion, he was able to only throw small vases on an electric wheel for a kitschy touristic ceramic studio in town. A year later, restored to robust good health, he was back working on his father's old manual kick wheel in the pottery he had established in the 1940s outside of town. I asked that he show me how to make a rabbina, a wine container unique to Sorano and the Porri family of potters. The pot was first designed and made by Luigino's great great great grandfather some 200 years before. It was commissioned by the wife of the Rabbino (Rabbi), thus the name, and was used in the town's synagogue. Both in my house and cantina along with a rabbina I have panatas in various sizes made by Luigino for dispensing wine and water. Two of my other prized possessions are a large olive oil urn and a decorated ceramic fire back in one of my fireplaces made by Luigino's great uncle Domenico.*

Luigino Porri making a rabbina in his studio

Back then we prepared our clay for the pottery. We would go to a place nearby. We would open the earth, take some clay and then leave it to dry in the sun. There it would dry. Then we would wet it in baths. We used the clay as it was. Sand would be added only in the case of making tiles for roofs etc. Nowadays this is all done with machines. It is all different. Our clay was better. We would go twenty kilometers with donkeys to collect the dried clay. Then we would soak it in baths. We would beat the clay with iron rods that were made especially for that purpose, but it was tiring work. We would do four trips a day to collect the clay. Not the clay from Sforzesca, but clay somewhat nearer—at Case Rocchi. The kiln was fired with wood, just like the ancient system. No electric wheel, nothing like that. Even now I use wood when I have to do my own things.

I would collect all the materials, and put them in that mill. I have one stone that is round and the other is in a crescent shape. It turns and grinds the materials. I would put in the silica and the red lead and mix them together. With the lead, we would heat it for eleven or twelve hours and then it would become powdery. It would then be milled. The old glaze was better than the pre-prepared ones. It was darker—a darker shade of yellow. To make the colors in the glazes, you use various other minerals. For green, you use copper—with the discarded bits of thick wire from the power lines I found in the dump. I would take the strands of copper, and put them in the oven, because the copper had to be heated to a higher temperature, like with the lead. The thicker wires had to be cooked twice. When it has been heated to a high temperature, it can be hit with a hammer or pestle to pulverize it, and then put in the mill and ground. The three colors we made were green, brown and black. Brown was made with another stone. It is against the law now to use lead. They say that it is bad for you, but it is not true. I don't believe it because I used it most of my life, and my grandfathers before me.

For my great grandfather, there was much work, because all the useful objects that all the families had, were made from pottery. In the houses, there were all the things of pottery. There were the big bowls where you washed vegetables. There was the washbowl for washing your face, the pitchers for carrying water, and colanders, etc. And then there were all the drainage pipes that you still see everywhere. After the war until about 1953, the use of these things really began to diminish. There was no longer any work. Plastic arrived. I quit as a potter and had to work as a builder.

The only piece of land I had is where the abandoned pottery is. Where the new pottery is, I bought the land. To eat, I bought everything. Except for us, the artisans, everyone had some land to support themselves upon. There, opposite my house, were all the terraces—they were all cultivated with vines. These were the vineyards. In all those little pieces of land were vines. Then down by the river they made little gardens where they grew potatoes, beans etc. But we grew nothing. All of us worked in the business. We lived on that.

Luigino

Here it was full of people—the families were numerous. So the men—they worked at the vineyards, and they would sit on the streets preparing the *ginestra* shoots to tie up the grape vines, or they would get hay for the donkeys. The women would do their things—all the lighter jobs. There wasn't gas or water. There was only the fireplace. One would make *polenta*. One went to the vineyard or garden, put together a bundle of sticks, and bring them back to make a little fire to cook on—also in summer.

Marietta

One would content oneself with the best way in which one could live: with the fireplace lit—with that which we could carry on life. The pigs. One would go to care for them in the stable. The women would do this. They would prepare the *beverone*—the swill for the pigs. Even just to provide for the pig was costly. The boys would go down to the river under the oak trees to collect acorns—to care for the pigs, and they would feed them the bad potatoes, and the apples that would otherwise be discarded. This was the life—you lived with these possibilities. There was nothing else. This is all before the war. During the period of fascism, there was propaganda for agriculture. So Mussolini encouraged the "*donne rurale*"—he sent the women these lovely scarves, on which it was written 'duce, duce, duce,' and these poor fools—*coglioni*—of our mothers who put on these scarves... But there are other things to say. That here in Tuscany, it is not as if Fascism was seen in a good light. Here in Sorano, there were ten cretins who went for the march on Rome. One was the street sweep, another was the watchman, and another was the banker. But then there was the imposition of the membership of fascism. Because there were the "little Italians." In the big cities, there were rallies. In the little towns, there was the *podesta*—the mayor—appointed by Mussolini. The authorities came from Grosseto. They planned processions. There was the day of October 22, 1922, that was a festival. They closed the schools, had a big demonstration in the piazza, with gymnastic displays because they considered gymnastics to be very important. We had to do gymnastics at school. This was inserted in the scholastic program.

Anyway, it happened this way: those that did not want to become members of the fascist movement were subversives. In '21 at Livorno, there was the schism between the Communists and the Socialists. In any event, they were all considered to be subversives, and they did not have the fascist membership card. In a little town like this, those that were anti-fascists were known. They did not have the card; they did not go to the demonstrations. So the Fascists came from the neighboring towns like Acquapendente or Viterbo, where Fascism was much more established. And they did things they should never have done. They beat up the Communists, and then sometimes they would give castor oil, which would make them vomit and have diarrhea. These were called the famous purges of Fascism. Then when there were these demonstrations with the banners, the Communists and Socialists would all disappear from the town. If not, then they would have been beaten. This happened until the War with Africa in '35 or '36 because Italy wanted to conquer its Empire. In fact, they did and "Italy finally has its Empire." Mussolini said these things. "Credere, obedire, combattere." Believe, obey, and fight. "Libri e moschetto Fascisto perfetto." Books and a musket make a Fascist perfect. These are the slogans that were written even on the walls. All the teachers, and the podesta were all indoctrinated and at school, we were required to do home work always. *Il Fascitorio*—our beloved duce and all these things were put in our heads. At home, we had problems because my father was anti-fascist. So we sang the Russian anthem, but we could not let them hear. Because if they heard there would have been big trouble.

There were families that had seven or eight children. Because the more children you had, the better. There was the rationing for those who were poor. So, the fascist regime would give a contribution—economic assistance if you had many children. If someone had some land, they were not considered poor enough to merit assistance.

PEPPINA

The laws of Mussolini—they did away with taxes for those that had more than seven children, because Mussolini wanted children. My family had eight children, but we continued to pay all the taxes because my father was a Communist and a very proud man. But Mussolini didn't know these things. If he had known he would really punish those that did not obey his orders. So, there was another law. A family would have a first and a second child. The third—*la terza*—like the others he should be eligible to be a soldier. But the first two were soldiers and the third no—why? Because it was the law. They sang, "*E tutti partono, e noi si resta, siamo di terza, siamo di terza...*" "And everyone leaves, and we stay behind, we are the third born, we are the third born." And I was the third born. There was Lorenzo and then Matusio. I did not have to serve as a soldier. Instead, not only did I serve, but so did my younger brother. We were all four of us fighting in that war. Mussolini would have punished my father if he had known that his law had been broken. He was a dictator, and his laws were the rule. He killed his father-in-law who didn't do as he wanted.

LEOPOLDO

On the 6th of June in 1940 Mussolini made a big speech at the palazzo Venezia that is remembered in history, when we finally entered the war. Also here in Sorano I remember that we all went—even those of us who did not want to go. Certainly the subversives, like my father, did not go. But we in school all had to go. Under the *palazzo communale,* the town hall, where they said that finally also Italy had declared war. In October our beloved Duce felt the need to go and bust the balls of the Greeks. The slogan was that we were going to break their back. Whereas it happened that our poor soldiers who went to fight without vehicles—with nothing—because we never had a military that was the least bit efficient, or that could measure up to other powers. Practically those that returned were destroyed, and many did not return at all. And we here suffered, but not like in the cities, because we had our loaf of bread, we had our potatoes, we had our pig, we had our chickens, and all that we harvested from the land. So although we may have felt hunger, it was not excessive. We had our ration card, and we got meat once a week. Certainly, we could not buy clothes or shoes because there weren't any. The farmers went to the fields with shoes made from tire treads. Instead of socks, you used rags. What happened was that many families returned to Sorano and other rural towns because conditions were better there than in the cities where people were dying of hunger. People who had left to find their fortunes were forced to return home. We took care of these relatives and friends with much affection. They stayed with us until the end of the war, because this war was not only fought on the fronts, it was fought all over. We passed the period of the war with much sadness. The teachers in school had us bring in wool pulled from the mattresses of our mothers, and from this wool, we made balaclava hats—even little children were set to work with knitting needles. It seemed that we were doing something very important. For us, it signified being near to our soldiers. Our soldiers who were up in the cold of Russia without shoes, and yet we thought we were going to win the war. At this time we came close to squalor—if it were cultural, economical or moral. We saw certain things that sometimes would make us numb. It is not as though the Germans did not come here—they were here. In certain caves, particularly on the road that comes up to the electrical transformer, they stored all their munitions. To prevent the Americans from seizing the munitions, they took them out and destroyed them—blew them up; enormous explosions that did considerable damage to the town. There were those houses that were very old, perhaps badly maintained, that were made more dangerous by these explosions. In this time it was very sad. We did not know which side we were on. Because there were the Germans and Austrians, and our soldiers were at war. At the house, there were only the old, the mothers and their children. To do the harvest, children ten years old went to do the work, because it was necessary. Women went with the men or in place of them to do all the hard work of plowing etc., just to be able to survive. We dressed as we could. Beds were covered with coats. We did not have covers—we were cold. We did not have the money to buy, nor even the merchandise to buy. This time we passed with distinct sadness—of poverty, of misery. There was much sickness. In the early forties, many youngsters died of tuberculosis. We had a lot of difficulties. We suffered the war.

When we arrived at '43 things went from bad to worse. When in July the Allies landed in Sicily, naturally our government could no longer stand. Badoglio went to the south. The King went into exile, and also he went naturally to the south. On the famous day of 8 September 1943 a new government was formed. This new government created chaos. Still, the Germans occupied the central north, and for this we found ourselves with the situation in the south, and in the north were the Germans who did not want to retreat. For this some of our men were deported to Germany. Others were fascists who continued to fight with the Germans, and then there were created the famous *Partigiani*. The partisans fought basically from '43 through to the end of the war. This was the worst period. From '43-'45. Nothing could be understood. There was much misery, sadness.

PEPPINA

After Mussolini fell, I quit. Essentially I was a deserter. I had to return to the forces, but I was saved because at the recruiting office where I reported in Grosseto there was a colonel from Sorano. He was a friend of my father, so when I went to regularize my military position I explained what I could only have done. I had found myself in command of a platoon of thirty soldiers. I called the command, but there was no one left—the officials had all fled. I said to the soldiers, save yourselves if you can. Every man for himself. I, as a Sergeant, could not command the platoon. So I returned home.

LEOPOLDO

After the eighth of September, many soldiers deserted, because the forces were shattered. Many soldiers returned at this point. The many that did not had already been sacrificed. They were prisoners or had died. When the partisan struggle began, we in Sorano were in a very worrying situation, because the boys that had returned from the war could not be revealed to the Germans—because the Germans refused to permit them to leave the army, to desert their posts. So, if they saw them, they would shoot them. There was one young man, Adamo Crisanti, who was hunted and shot down in the middle of the town. For us, in this little place, it was a real tragedy to see one of our own, our friend, and playmate killed—he was no more than twenty. These were the laws of war, and there was nothing to do about it. The fascists on the one side, and the partisans on the other. The Jews deported. Families split. We passed a period where people did not even have the will to speak.

PEPPINA

To avoid going as a prisoner with the Americans when he was down in Sicily, my husband escaped. And he was never discharged—or granted permission. After fighting for three years in Sicily, without ever returning, without writing for a year. Finally, a postcard arrived. Imagine how he was always in my thoughts. My father, who was working for the local government, said that he was missing. He asked how long it was since I had heard from him. I said that the last postcard was from the twenty-fifth of July 1943, when they went ashore in Sicily. And in that postcard he wrote: "I am at the Villa San Giovanni. I am well." He was already out of Sicily—he had already passed the Straits of Messina. With that postcard I was put at ease, but there was no more news after that. So my father in the end received news that he was missing. As it happened, although I would have been happy if he was in America— better there than somewhere else as prisoner—he was a deserter. He got over the Straits of Messina with his lieutenant on a raft. At this point I heard nothing more for thirteen months. That postcard that came from Calabria meant that he was not a prisoner. But, because he was a deserter he could not come home, so he stayed with a family in Brindisi. And letters did not get through. He could not show himself here until the line had passed to the north. When he heard that our area had been taken he slowly made his way up by foot from Taranto. He arrived at ten in the evening from the valley below—from Onano by foot, without shoes and dressed only in a pair of shorts. But it was thirteen months that I had not heard whether he was dead or alive. Angiolina, the sister of Gino, came to me and said that my fiancé had arrived at ten during the curfew. I went to see him, and when we came back, the door was locked, with the key inside. We had to get a ladder to get back inside. It was July, and everyone was sleeping with their windows open. In the morning we had to make the bread.

MATILDE

If they had found me, they would have shot me, so I stayed for some time in a cave. I lived there well enough, even though my father thought I would be sick. At night I had to extinguish the fire. After some time a man with a large farmhouse that at the time was secluded, and where much of the new town was eventually built, offered me a room. By ten at night, I would go there and sleep. He gave me a bed in his house. It then seemed that I had an obligation towards this man, so I married

Ivana, *until the death of her husband a few years ago, had never traveled more than five miles from Sorano. Before my return to New York on one occasion she asked if I was going to drive there. I often visit with Ivana as I buy olive oil from her, or have her hem curtains or knit a hat for me. She is tough and resourceful. Despite debilitating operations on both knees she continues to hobble down with her crutch to the valley and tend to her garden by the river. We always chat, but on the day that I interviewed her, we stood at the wall in front of her home looking onto the valley and at the dirt path that for centuries had been the route into town for everyone and their donkeys coming from the surrounding hamlets. Coming up from the river, it passes under one of the medieval gates. From the Porta dei Merli, the way is cobblestoned and winds up past one of the old potteries, and then into the town proper. Recently, the pottery was bought and restored as a home by a German family. On the roof where pots had traditionally been placed to dry in the sun two middle aged Germans were lying out in bikinis for all the town to see. Vasco came and joined us. Like Ivana born in 1930, as a baby of eight months, he had meningitis and lost his hearing. He taught himself to speak, but it is quite difficult to understand him. Other than being known for having used black boot polish to dye his hair until he poisoned himself, he is also famous for his excellent ability to do slapstick mimed impersonations of some of the town characters. When I pointed out the view below he was immediately inspired to drop his trousers, wave them around his head, yodel and strut about in his underwear doing leg kicks like a Radio City Rockette. We all three of us collapsed with laughter. The only other place Ivana had been to with one of her sons and grandchildren was the seaside resort of Rimini. "There you can lie about in a bikini," she exclaimed, "or on the television, you see these things because there nothing is real." She particularly likes to watch Santa Barbara. But never had she seen something like this in Sorano. It just does not seem right, she said.*

Ivana Castrini

his daughter. Not because... I had many. She is eight years younger than me. That evening she fell in love with me like a cat. I had loves, but the real one died under the bombardment of Rome.

I have saved Jews. I saved a Jewish man and woman who had the fascists on their tails, and who would have caught them. Servi was their name. I knew the area well and found them in a ditch. I said, "*Porca Madosca*[4] you are the Servi?" And they said yes—you know us. I said that I knew that they were from Pitigliano, and they said that the Germans had come to take them away from there. I said where I will take you nobody will find you, and if they do show their faces I have a rifle and will make mincemeat out of them. She now is in America. When she returns she comes to find me and embraces me. At least three times I have seen her. She would say to her husband, "If I kiss this man it doesn't mean anything because he saved my life."

Another time there was an air battle between the Americans and the Germans. There were flying fortresses ready to bomb, but the Germans were shooting them up so the American bombers let go their fuel tanks. There were many dead. I saw two parachutists that came down. I was near where I had saved the Jews, and with my rifle. The men put up their hands and said that they were Americans. I could see that they were Americans. These two Americans I could not understand. It was night, so I left them sleeping in a cave. The night after, I took them to Onano—fifteen kilometers away. In Onano I had a friend who thought like me, a friend of my father, who had lived in America and spoke English. He was known as "*Dente D'Oro*"—Gold tooth. At the time there were rations, and it was a real sacrifice to feed them. They were very tall these aviators. "What beasts you brought me," said *Dente*

---

[4] *Porca madosca* is a *bestemmia*—one of many blasphemous expletives commonly employed by Tuscans when either surprised or annoyed. In this case, Leopoldo uses madosca as a euphemism for the Madonna, so it is not quite so offensive, but the essential meaning is that the Madonna is a pig. Leopoldo's brother Mario was particularly inventive with the use of the bestemmia. One of his more notable utterances was "*Dio cane con dente d'avorio*," meaning a deified dog with a smile of pearly whites—an almost likeable image. When I first came to Italy, I spent most of my time around crusty old communists and hardened builders, and so my Italian was liberally peppered with *bestemmie*—until a more decorous person pointed out to me that speaking that way really is decidedly rude.

D'Oro. Porca Madosca! For five months they stayed at his house until the front passed. Every so often I would go with my bicycle to see how they were doing. When they left, they shook Dente D'Oro's hand and said goodbye to me through him. No thanks, no postcard—nothing. From that point, I was disgusted, if not from the bombings, but this.

Leopoldo

There was a terrible bombardment with flying fortresses, and there was an air battle. One American came down with his parachute, landed on the plain, and then went into a thicket. This small thicket belonged to the father of Mariuccia. Our piece of land bordered with theirs. Just imagine, my father would go there every day, and never saw this man. He never knew that Mariuccia would bring Lieutenant Arturo food to eat, his clean laundry, the things he needed. For me, my father said, that man did not exist. He was there for three years until the front passed north of here, and he rejoined the troops. He gave many gifts—a watch and a bracelet to Mariuccia—before he left. Then he disappeared. But he must have died, as the front went on to the north of Italy. Because he was a lovely man and it seems impossible that he did not send a postcard. There was another soldier who stayed with another family—there were two of them. That one wrote from America. And to think, with that great risk—because the Germans, of course, they were here when that fellow came down with his parachute. If they had known, they would have shot everyone.

Assunta

When the war ended on the twenty-fifth of April, we were liberated of everything. The euphoria was such that we all seemed mad. It seemed that everything had to return to normal. But we in this little town were unaware how devastated the cities were—that the economy was destroyed and that the industries were not functioning. There was nothing left. We were left in our little Sorano the same. From this point, we had to start from the beginning.

Peppina

When my sister was married in 1945, you could not find shoes. So my father went out and killed some snakes. They were skinned. Then they were tanned with alum. The leather was thin, but he was able to make shoes out of them. Errigo Goscioni made the shoes. She went on her honeymoon wearing serpent shoes!

Assunta

There was nothing during or after the war. You had to shine your shoes with pot black. Before everyone was ingenious. Now no one knows how to do anything—then there was the necessity to be clever. Before, to feed the pigs, they would go to pick nettles. Now the troughs are full.

Matilde

In '46 the Republic was founded, there were elections, and we had the first government of Gasparri. There were many innovations. Pensions were established so that the old people who got by with their cup of milk, in which they dipped their bread, could survive reasonably well until their death. Here they established the *scuole magistrale*, and other schools over time.

Peppina

In addition to the houses they did an agrarian reform. Instead of working land which they did not own, L'Ente Maremma (the Maremma Association) gave land to everyone. Nowadays everyone has their land to do with as they wish. To raise pigs, to work the earth. The state declared that all the lands *malcolti e malcoltivati* (incorrectly seized and poorly cared for) could be expropriated. So the lands were taken from the big landowners like the Ricci/Busatti. In the beginning, like in an invasion, the left provoked the people to confiscate the lands. Immediately after the war, they took the lands over, a piece for each. They did it as bullies would. They said this land is ours—we did this war for you? Do we need to threaten you? We need to eat. What did Busatti say? I'll tell you. He spoke with a representative, a little old man, by the name of Luigi Picchini. Picchini went to ask him if he would give up his farm. He explained that at least the Soranese wished him well. You know how he responded? "Better a liter of blood than a clod of earth." You understand? He preferred to live, and they took everything. But, once the government declared the law, they took the lands both from him and from the occupiers, and then redistributed it again.

In the beginning, I worked for the cooperative as a buyer. At first with the invasion of the lands, then with the land distribution, and then with the cooperative—and I got nothing (*un cazzo.*) One person got a farm, another some land and me nothing, *Dio Animale.* Afterward, I began my political career. At that time the Christian-Democrat party was founded, and I was hoping to get something out of it—those bastards. Then it went badly: I was backed up by the Left, because there was the cooperative. After, I put myself up to be the town counselor, at the time of the first mayor in 1945. There were mayors before the war. But at the time of the fascists, they were canceled. During that time there was the *podesta*, which was nominated by the state. It was said that the fascists nominated *chi gli garbava, chi menava e chi purgava* (those they liked, those who threatened and those who purged.) To those that did not think like them, they gave castor oil. So, I was counselor, and then I was mayor for a couple of years, and then I was an assessor for a while, until they busted my balls and then I quit.

MICHELE

After the war fascism fell, etcetera, etcetera, but Italy remained still under the fascists because the Christian-Democrats were voted in. The fascists—those that commanded—were passed into the Christian-Democrats, and we had to suffer the consequences. The Christian-Democrats did *L'Ente Maremma*—an agrarian reform, according to them. So from these little pieces of land that we created, they made them larger and then gave them to whomever they wanted. For me, it would have been enough to have that little piece that I occupied, but it was taken away, and I was given nothing more. To some of the other Communists who cooperated they gave larger shares. So these shares they have were enlarged, but mindful of the people that they gave them to. If they were Christian-Democrat aligned, then they got some—if Communist they got nothing.

When they had the election, for example—in America they told you the opposite. After the war, the *Partita Communista* would have won with an absolute majority. Those from southern Italy would have all voted Communist. I had twenty of them under my command as a sergeant during the war. Afterward, they told me that they had to vote Christian-Democrat. All of the powerful people were with the Mafia. They gave people ballots already filled out for Andreotti and the Christian-Democrats—those that the Mafia wanted. The lousy Socialists made a pact with the Christian-Democrats and won the election. Also, always meddling were the priests who told the women how to vote. They said to the women, "you will go to hell if you vote for the Communists." So it was necessary to be vigilant with them. And even now as much as ever. With the Pope let's not joke. Watch the television and look at what type of retribution! He can't bring himself to say that the nearby Madonna of Cerreto, two kilometers from Sorano, is like that of Fatima in Portugal because he wants that my wife wants desperately to go to Fatima, and he wants from me one million lire to send her down there. He should say, "Signora, don't go down there because the Madonna of Cerreto is the same as that of Fatima," and the same as in most other places. Am I right or not? I cannot tolerate these things. This is how they won. And this is where I have them (he points to his throat) the priests, the monks, the Christian-Democrats, all the Capitalists, all Americ.... And when I hear about a rich man my blood boils. Because

I went around in cars and visited the farmers. The rich owners of the land kept the record books. Ninety % of the farmers were illiterate, and so the owners cooked the books. At the end of the month, they were always in the red. Never at the end of the year did they say, "Here is an extra quintal of grain." Never... he was always in debt. And if someone complained, he was sent away from the farm. And where would he go? Here is the life of the Christian-Democrats. I am Communist, I will stay Communist, and I will die Communist. Now everyone has shit on their face, because some became Socialists—switched for money, etcetera. If not we would have gone under the Communists, and then we would have set everything straight for good.

Leopoldo

Before there was no political activity. Ideologically everyone was equal in a simple way. Essentially the Church ruled, because a member of the rich families always was either a bishop or a *monsignore*. Now the situation is that there is some animosity—some Communists will not come to this bar, and will only go to the other bar. But twenty years ago it was worse. If you were a Communist, you were a bandit. Only nowadays do the Communists have the same rights, and can be accepted as the others. Twenty years ago, families were torn apart by ideology. After the war, the fascists having been disposed of, there were the Communists, the Socialists and the anti-Communists/Socialists (the Christian-Democrats) that represented the Catholic Church. Later the Socialists allied themselves with the Christian-Democrats. But, this being a country made up primarily of Catholics, with considerable influence from the Vatican, the Communists were never able to win a majority.

Michele

Leopoldo *is, for me, the most gracious and friendly brother of the Mari family. He served as a go-between and advisor in the buying of a family property that they had used as a granary. He may have been assigned the task of dealing with me, the foreigner, as his daughter some years before had married a Swede. I found it disconcerting that he would clear his throat and spit with apparent great distaste at the conclusion of our many meetings. But, without his suggestions as how to handle each uniquely challenging member of the notoriously difficult family, I likely would never have been able to sign the deed. The granary became the first of two small rooms I renovated and lived in as I fixed up the rest of my home. Poldo*  agreed *to let me interview him at his cantina, which is in one of the many caves lining the winding road that leads to the southeast out of town. I had been painting my ceiling and arrived by bike spattered with the day's efforts. As we spoke, he angrily prod me in the chest to make his points, and then, almost embarrassed by his fervor, would gently pick pieces of dried lime from my shirt. He spoke primarily of his own specific grievances against the injustices of the Fascists and Christian-Democrats. Sometimes he was so enraged that it seemed that I was his hated Fascista, the hated Maresciallo, the hated Capitalista, the hated Americano. Many like him consider the Americans responsible for having perpetuated for decades the corrupt ruling coalition of the Christian-Democrats and Socialists. Yet, he would alternately ease up and suggest that perhaps "I thought like he did." Perhaps I gained his confidence by expressing my interest in traditional life, and by making wine, but his mistrust remains unallayed. The day after the interview he came to me and asked that I destroy the photographs I had taken of him. He was genuinely concerned that his irate opinions might result in some retribution against his family by far right followers of the ruling POLO coalition, headed by Prime Minister Berlusconi. Since then the left for the first time since the Second World War has won a majority in parliament, so I hope his fears are no longer so great.*

In places like Sorano, politics is understood in a very strange way. Because any doctrine, be it Catholic, Marxist or whatever is an ideology. So it is not easy to make others have respect for divergent ideologies. You with your ideology, and me with mine. We cannot afford to be extremists because as we know, the times have changed. That which we are doing in Sorano is not finished. Our leaders have argued in the Senate and the House. They argue on television. Ideology did not exist before because we were not in the position to have an ideology. Those who maintain that before we were united, and now we are not, are wrong. In Sorano, there has always been the difference of class. All it took was to have a little store where you sold a hectogram of mortadella and a hectogram of jam, and then you could put on your little hat. The daughter of a peasant could not put on that hat and had to walk behind the tail of the donkey. Those that felt superior or considered themselves to be of a superior class—if they had been working for the town hall, or had their shop—they are the ones who support the right. However, everything begins from the economic standpoint. I don't say that they have to be Communists, or have to be Christian-Democrat. I say that they have to be that which they are. Your liberty cannot begin where mine ends. It is necessary that we conquer liberty together.

PEPPINA

I was at this point simply a road worker. I was not yet even a foreman, because someone always put a wrench in the works—because I was a Communist. And the administration was run by those that I have already talked about. In all honesty, an engineer came to me and told me to throw away my membership card. "What the hell do you care?" How could I throw away my card in front of the other workers? I always had faith and my conscience. I worked ten years as a road worker, and I was not promoted because I was a Communist. So those people prepared a complicated preliminary plan for the work. But I said that the problem was simple. So, I said, "Mr. Engineer, this is a very simple problem." Here you need some chestnut beams. Beginning from below, steps are made with these beams; it is all filled up with earth and with acacia seeds. If this were a problem with my land, I would do it like this. So the engineer said, "Listen all of you, tomorrow I am sending these beams to him, and you all take orders from him." There were twenty road workers there, and they were all put to my service. I did as I had suggested and the road has stayed there from that time 'til now. From that point, the engineer had great faith in me and, little by little, word passed from one to another. They made me the assistant, and I earned my money with good work and good fortune.

LEOPOLDO

The new houses were constructed at the end of the fifties. Here in this square was a landslide, aside from the hole, which happened in '54 or '55. There was a sinkhole because a sewer pipe broke, and so there was a slide. They brought the issue before the court. I was there as well because I was the town assessor at the time. They saw a way to say that the area was giving way. With the excuse of the landslide, they were able to get money from the government. The houses were constructed, and the people were moved up to the new town. From the moment that they left is the end of the story of these people who had sacrificed themselves by living in stables and holes. They were pulled out of those holes. New apartments were rented to all these people, and they got homes like they had never had before. Their parents—all the old people had never seen such nice houses like these.

I will tell you why the one side was abandoned. There was a sewer in the Manfredo Vanni Piazza. This sewer broke and created a sink hole—a big hole in the square. So they took the ball as it was bouncing and moved half the town.

There was already a decree from 1927 to transfer the people because it was considered an unstable zone—but it was never carried out, and the people stayed there. So in 1959-60, we profited from the sinkhole. We did a televised event of a propagandistic nature because Sorano was in danger. For this, we communicated to the entire world that Sorano was collapsing.

MICHELE

Those that left the village below left because they were sent away. Those houses that were done afterward were different—done in a different way, because of course before there were no toilets—nothing like that. But, a house fell. The house fell because the owners went away. It was abandoned. Houses, when they are abandoned the beams rot, etcetera, etcetera. The house collapsed, and in came the civil engineers. He said that the house fell off its foundations, because of the river. Where they poked at it, maybe a few rocks fell, but underneath the tufo foundations of the village do not move. Allow me at least this, because I wasn't born yesterday.

LEOPOLDO

This was not a decision made by the people here. It was the civil engineers from Grosseto who said that they had to go away from there. They did not want to leave, but they were forced to do so. You remember poor Mario Mari. Mario did not want to go away. The carabinieri came to take him away, but he would not go.

LUIGINO

When the sinkhole occurred, however, they took advantage of the situation because the people wanted to go away—and this was right. I maintain that it was right that the people were pulled out of there because we cannot leave five or six people inside a room with donkeys and pigs. So it was not in regard to geological stability, but in regard to social rights, because these people had to be moved to this other place.

When Prime Minister Fanfani came to Sorano in 1962, he gave

ten million lire to begin work on the new houses.[5] Everyone then was squatting because with that propaganda and the help of the carabinieri they had pulled everyone out. They put them where they could, like in the school—that was once the villa of the Busatti family up in the fortress. So they began to build that big housing complex for those people.

MICHELE

Yes, they decided to make the new houses, where I worked as a builder for two years. The Borgo part of the town was totally abandoned as the houses were constructed. But I think most went away voluntarily from here because the new houses were more modern. There was more space—they were larger. They would pay a rent, a certain sum each month. Eventually, they were sold to the renters. After some twenty years.

LUIGINO

While many Soranese have gone to the cities to be doormen, or workers—to do many types of types artisan work etc—in Sorano people who previously lived in the surrounding villages came to town. So we are no longer pure Soranese here—being from the same social extraction. These are people that we no longer know, like those whom we had known since we were born. Here in Sorano, those originally from Sorano are very few. So those that have come from outside don't have the localisms that we have. The people who have the general store are from Montebuono. The photographer is from Elmo. The town surveyor is from Elmo. Others are from San Quirico, and yet others from San

---

[5] Prime Minister Fanfani came to Sorano and gave a televised address to the nation. Unfortunately, Sorano became a model for future development in Italy. The message was that it was much more efficient and less costly to build new apartments than to renovate the old villages.

Valentino. The people who run the pizzeria are from Rome. The proprietor of the restaurant is not from Sorano. The few of us that remain are tied to each other, by our shared experiences, living together—and by our mothers and grandparents. It has all changed. It is not as it once was. And it has also changed because we once were much more humble, modest, and more submissive. Now progress has also arrived here. We are equal, whether it is the son of the doctor, or the pharmacist, or of the Marshall. But, progress has also brought us degeneration, because nothing pleases us anymore. We should return somewhat to our origins. Why do parents have only one or two children nowadays? Because they fear that they can no longer afford them—to pay for their education, to buy them cars.

PEPPINA

When we grew up no one studied, or at most to the fifth grade—we were asses. Now they go to school, and they are asses all the same. And they don't respect their parents. People do not have respect because everyone considers themselves big shots. They have everything, as compared with in the past, and they are totally dissatisfied with what they have. If a grandmother gave a dried fig, it was too much. And then they would send us out with two *soldi*. One *soldo* for one anchovy, and the other *soldo* for one herring. The more that there is, the less one is happy. We had nothing.

MATILDE

When we lived down here, there was no television. It came later. The first television that I saw was in another town in '52. But the television in Sorano was only here in my workshop. The people came to see this one. Here there were all the seats. This place was a bar before, and this the television room. The people came up here, almost as though it was a cinema. During the evenings it was full.

Luigino

Before there was little contact with the outside world, and the town of Sorano made do on its own—it did not get money from the state. There was the family tax, the animal tax, the tax on buildings, and the tax on lands. With these taxes, they kept going—before the war, and a bit after. Before, there were no debts, as they would put in the bank that which they took in, and took that which they needed for expenses. So for this, there were those communities that went well and those that went badly. The first time you saw a train was when you went away for military service. When you were a soldier that was when you began to see the world. Before the First World War few people went away because there had been no such wars. They began to see things. Most everything that changed happened after 1945. The revolution happened then. This previously was an isolated post. Those that went into the service went to the cities, to emigrate there and seek out work. Only a few distanced themselves from here, however. The majority remained here. That with which you entertained yourself was here. They danced. One diverted oneself here. Snacks in the cantina. Now they just go elsewhere.

Michele

Here no one likes living in the country, so everyone has gone away. They have gone to different ports. Before we were all rooted to the land. One produced from the earth the little that one needed. One ate and contented oneself with the little that one had. As boys, we would go to the cantinas and have parties. Everyone had his or her circle of friends. *È cosi era la vita.* And such was life. No one had money, and as I have already said, my grandfather and we, his family, could live on his little pension. I used to go around with my friends, four or five always together. We would ask each other how much money we had. "I have a *ventino*"—four *soldi*. We saw if we could have a game and if there was enough for everyone to have a drink. We had a life like this. Life has changed from this to that (indicates by showing his palm and then turning over his hand), but it could have changed better.

LEOPOLDO

So, before there was nothing—*via*. There weren't comforts, in sum. Now it is worse perhaps because there is no one. All these houses are empty. Now they come during summer for a month. Instead, before there were so many people—perhaps too many. In my family, I was the oldest, although the firstborn Mario died at eighteen months. Three of my mother's ten children died very young. The last, Vasco was born when my mother was forty-two, and he died fifteen days later. I am thirteen years older than Annetta. There are few of us left. You know how many years I have counted to this point? Eighty-five. What am I doing here? It is time for me to die.

MARIETTA

Marietta Savelli
1911-1996

...and fiercely my heart aches
To think how everything in this world passes
And leaves no trace. For look, the holiday
Is over now, an ordinary day
follows; all things our race has known
Time also bears away. Where now is the voice
Of the ancient peoples, the clamor of our ancestors?...
All is peace and quiet; the world is still;
And no word now remains of them.

"THE EVENING OF THE HOLIDAY" (1819)

The slow tolling of Sorano's church bells fills November's empty streets. The somber series of three peals in descending order of pitch declares a death, and then again, within the next days, calls family and friends to the funeral service. With the crowds of summer gone, and the brisk activity of the *vendemmia* (the making of wine that permeates the town in October with the aroma of fermenting grapes) over, November is an uncertain time. The weather alternately is dominated by the *ponente,* a westerly wind that often brings heavy rains and leaden skies, and the *tramontana,* a frigid northerly that blows hard down from the Alps. The days of this seasonal struggle, and its inevitable wintry outcome, are increasingly marked by the deaths of the weak and infirm.

The bells mean there will be one less man to make wine next year—his meager plot of land abandoned and overgrown—or one less woman making her slow way about the piazza, buying the ingredients for the day's meal or sitting and chatting with her friends—her house shuttered and silent. Births are rare and do little to counteract the decline of the population in terms of numbers, and nothing in terms of memory or culture.

On November 12, 1996, the ringing of the bells was interrupted by power outages. Terrific thunderstorms the previous day had caused a landslide, which knocked over an electricity pylon. The solemnity of the moment, as I was preparing to attend my first funeral after eight years in Sorano, was repeatedly broken by long silences between the mournful knells. I was working in my cantina at the time, preparing to drain my new wine from the barrels and discard the lees, and these interruptions provoked exasperated thoughts and whimsical musing: frustration with the electrical company, whose primitive service meant that I had to keep candles in ample supply, and whimsy with the idea that the pauses might somehow have been Marietta Savelli's last hurrah. But Marietta's eighty-five years had been hard, so it was a mistake to imagine that she might have wanted to forestall her passage.

When I arrived at the church piazza, several people were gathered outside despite a fine drizzle. Many were ex-Communists, and the rest uninterested in hearing the cleric's all-too-familiar high-pitched redundant sermonizing. The rectangular thirteenth-century church, the Chiesa di San Niccolò, built with volcanic tufo blocks and topped by a Romanesque travertine bell tower, is unremarkable except for the heavy chestnut doors adorned by the petals of large carved roses. I walked through one of the side doors of the vestibule and stood at the back of the whitewashed nave. The last time I had been inside the church was only a week before. As I was running back from the piazza in a driving rainstorm, Giuseppe asked me to help carry a coffin containing his aged aunt from the town hearse to the altar. Giuseppe's brother, Navio, had earlier in the year sold me his two large chestnut tubs to ferment my wine in. Although I never heard him, I have been told that Navio was a very good mandolin player. He lived nearby me, and I knew him as being sad (particularly after the then recent death of his wife), drunk, and hunchbacked. Navio had died only a couple of weeks before his aunt, and oddly enough his father, an intelligent and knowledgeable ninety-six-year-old, passed with him the same day.

The priest droned at the numerous mourners, who came mostly from Sorano but also from Rome, Viterbo, and Grosseto. Funerals are much better attended than Sunday Masses, and Carlone was making his methodical way among the pews, collecting donations. Carlone is an idiot savant who knows the birthday of everyone in town, including my own. He also knows the day of any date in history. If he is asked what day was January 3, 1752, he will tell you accurately that it was a Monday. When at the town cemetery, which he goes to frequently as he leads all funeral processions carrying a large cross before him, he is known to wander from plot to plot muttering the names of the relatives of the deceased, and their various dates of death. Otherwise, Carlone seems simpleminded, and the townspeople use him to run errands and carry heavy objects, like cooking-gas cylinders, that need to be delivered here and there. He is a stocky troll of a man, with a low gravelly voice and large hairy ears.

Pietro Barbini

I soon rejoined the Communists outside and sat on a low wall facing the church with Carlone's sister, Peppina. An urbane and opinionated woman, she made telling comments about the proceedings and spoke of Marietta's sad and onerous life, her spartan ways, and the event that had precipitated her decline. Over many years Marietta had saved her pension payments, and being distrustful, as many old widows are, she kept her savings hidden in her bedroom closet under some linen. She had planned to give the sum, estimated to be about fifty million lire ($32,000) to her great-nephew on his wedding day. After the money was stolen in April, she no longer trusted anyone; she became reclusive, gnawed at by her fears and suspicions. Everyone who lived nearby her was accused—a Roman brother of a neighbor, a previously jailed

Genovese builder, a Venetian heroin addict, and even her best friend, also named Marietta. The two Mariettas, who were about the same age, would often walk arm in arm up to the piazza and sit together with other friends by one of the bronze lion-headed fountains in the piazzetta at the entrance to the old town. The wicked word around town was that Marietta's own family had arranged the robbery.

I left Peppina talking with Matusio, one of the nine Mari relations from whom I bought one of my properties, to join a cluster of old men a few feet away. We had not been able to drink or cook with tap water in Sorano for the previous day, as the reservoir, supplied by water from the Fiora River, had apparently been contaminated by a toxic fuel spill. The old men's discussion was about obtaining potable water, and how the situation was not unlike thirty years before, when families had to go with containers to a fountain. I spoke first with Augusto, citified and precise in his tweed suit, and amusingly ardent about his two passions—grappa and women. Talking of alternate beverages, he recently had been to a bar near his home in Viterbo and had tasted an exceptional grappa flavored with nettle. He heard that I had made a rather good grappa with pear, and he was eager to try it.

Gino, the brother of Marietta's long-deceased husband, wanted to know how the recipe he told me for *grappa al limone* had turned out. I had to admit that it was too sweet, but he assured me that this was easily corrected by adding more pure grappa. He asked me when I was planning to return to the United States, and I was able to say that I would be back in time for Thanksgiving, a holiday he remembered well from his days as a POW during the Second World War. Leopoldo, Matusio's brother, began loudly denouncing President Clinton for failing to deal fairly with Fidel Castro, so I turned to speak with him. Despite the inverted name, when Warren Christopher was named as Secretary of State in 1993, I automatically became the resident expert—and whipping board—on US foreign policy. Gossip had it that he is in fact my uncle, thus making me privy to the darkest secrets of the US State Department.

Castro was in Rome at the time, attending a United Nations meeting on worldwide hunger. One of the day's headlines was that the fabulously wealthy capitalist and chairman of Fiat, Giovanni Agnelli, had Castro to dinner the evening before. I pointed out the irony of Castro attending a sumptuous feast, considering the occasion of his visit to Italy, and said also that Agnelli's intention clearly was to butter him up so he can build more Fiat factories. Poldo's pleased response was that the factories would be good for employment in Cuba. My riposte was, of course, that Agnelli, too, would be pleased, as wages there are so low. I playfully suggested that Agnelli should perhaps have prepared Castro's pasta with water from the Fiora, which Poldo thought was particularly tasteless and let me know by bobbing the back of his hand in my face, thumb and forefingers pressed together.

With a resounding tintinnabulation, the service came to an end. Gino was playing happily with his young grandson, as Pacifico, who doubled as the greengrocer, pulled the hearse up to the front of the church. Among the mourners, Carlone emerged wearing a high-collared, starched white shirt and an askew black tunic. He went to the front of the procession, holding the Christ figure on the cross, impatiently glancing about and talking to himself. Brothers and nephews placed the coffin into the back of the hearse, while the priest, after a furtive look at the rain now pouring from an ash-gray sky, folded up his umbrella, hitched up his long black skirts, and slipped into the front passenger seat. Sixty or so persons made up the procession, and we began the slow walk up to the cemetery.

From the small church piazza we proceeded along what had been the main street in the old town. Fourteenth-to-sixteenth-century buildings rise four or five stories above the narrow street. Their facades were plastered and painted with sometimes quite elaborate decoration and trompe l'oeil effects. The once brilliant colors have now faded, and patches of the plaster have fallen away, revealing the chipped tufo below. Strips of gray cement show where tracks for sewage pipes had been cut into the walls. Rooms at street level had been primarily shops for merchandise and services, but along the 150-yard stretch from the church to the medieval entrance to the town, only five continue to be used as such.

In the previous year the pharmacy had moved to the new town, and Graziella, proprietor of the last food store in the old town, retired. Thirty-five years before, there was the same pharmacy, but also another church, four barbers, two ironsmiths, two joiners, three cobblers, six food shops, two butchers, two fruit and vegetable stores, a milk vendor, a jewelry shop, two clothing stores, three cloth merchants, two tobacconists, a furniture store, a cantina and *frantoio* (where wine and olive oil were made and sold), an agricultural supply association, four bars, a *caffetteria* (which had moved into the town's synagogue in the 1920s), a flea market, a large emporium (a few years later to become the movie theater), a *trattoria*, and a hotel. On this day Agata closed up her general store while the procession passed—as did Walter the antiquarian, Giorgio the joiner, and Patrizia the tanner—so the deserted street reverberated only with shuffling feet and muffled remarks.

We slowed briefly as the crowd funneled towards the old town's egress, and I looked up at the familiar inscription above the arch, painted in large black letters on a white background, and still legible despite being halfheartedly scratched out: ITALIA HA FINALMENTE IL SUO IMPERO. (Italy Finally Has Its Empire), signed Benito Mussolini. We walked out into the part of town that was built up at the end of the nineteenth century, and where, in the 1950s and 1960s, most of the stores moved. The first piazzetta is defined by a semi-ovate wall, with five bronze lion heads squirting water into bronze scallop shells, travertine benches—that Marietta and others would sit on, changing from one to the next as the sun moved on its course—and three small arched openings in the wall to look out west and down onto the Lente River valley.

Just beyond the piazzetta, a stairway leads down to a now disused large circular public washtub. The short stretch of road is bordered by buildings that contain the town bakery and newsagent on one side, and the offices of an architect and a bank on the other. The town's main square, the Piazza del Municipio, is on a relatively steep 10 percent slope. The low end is flanked by the Communist bar to the left and the Socialist—now "Berlusconi"—bar (named after the head of the right-wing political alliance and current prime minister) to the right. Here several members of the funeral party surreptitiously splintered off to their bars of choice, and the cortege, reduced by a quarter, continued up the length of the piazza. The town hall and post office are on the western side, and most of the town's shops are opposite, with a row of plane trees between them, running down the center. Towards the high end, a handful of mourners drifted over to the last of the piazza's three bars. This is the Fascist bar, most likely so-named because another of

Mussolini's inscriptions was painted above it: NOI ERAVAMO GRANDI QUANDO ALTRI POPOLI NON ERANO NATI. (We Were Great When Other Peoples Did Not Yet Exist.) A more sinister slogan directly faced the town hall: *The Italian People Has Created By Its Blood the Empire. It Will Propagate Through Its Work and Will Defend Itself Against Anyone With Its Weapons.*

The rain fell harder as we made our way up out of the piazza, making a 300-degree right turn at the walls of the twelfth-century fortress and proceeding for another two hundred yards until we came to a crossroads. Only about half of the original party turned left and continued on to the cemetery. The others went straight ahead and to the right, returning to their homes in the new town. We walked up onto the plain above Sorano. I looked onto the piazza, a hundred vertical yards below, and the medieval town with the principal Via Roma at its center, houses proceeding down on either side of the ridge, halfway to the river—abandoned side to the west, and the side that I live on to the east. Few people spoke, their heads down against the rain. Franca, the wife of Pacifico, and Peppina were not particularly interested that this was to be my first visit to the cemetery.

A high wall encloses the cemetery, and the wide square entrance was crowded with small groups of people talking among themselves, shaking rain from their coats and fiddling with their umbrellas while they waited to see Marietta's family at the far end. Once the coffin had been positioned opposite Marietta's chamber, the throng moved into the inner courtyard. At the center of the courtyard are individual plots with headstones, some dating back two hundred years. In the 1940s the town constructed above-ground tombs that appear as walls, two coffin-lengths thick and five high, surrounding the old graves and radiating from them. At the front of each chamber a small oval photograph of the deceased is affixed to the marble facing, which is set slightly into the wall, leaving a ledge for flowers and religious paraphernalia. Marietta was to be placed in a fourth-tier chamber, and everyone was crammed into the narrow alley between two walls of vaults. The coffin was up on a forklift and could not be placed into its space because of another power outage. Marietta's sister, Annetta, walked away from the commotion, and I joined her. She took some of the funerary flowers and went to the other side of the cemetery, where she showed me the vaults that contain Marietta's husband and son, and further on those of her mother and father. She asked me at each to empty the dead flowers from the vases and refill them with water and the fresh flowers that she had trimmed with trembling hands.

After the problem with the forklift was resolved and the coffin was in its chamber, most people stayed around to visit the tombs of friends and relatives. Peppina took me to the tombs of her father and mother, and then I accompanied Maria Torrants to the final resting place of her father, who had come to Sorano from Barcelona shortly after the First World War. Eventually I walked back to town alone. When I came to the crossroads I went straight on and then almost immediately turned right down a shorter and much steeper road to the piazza.

The storm had passed, the sun was setting quite magnificently, and I could hardly avoid thinking about Marietta and others like her who die, they and their knowledge, savvy, and experience soon forgotten, when I was aroused by a hearty yell from one of the several cantinas that line the road. *"Cristofe, vieni qui a prendere un bicchiere!"* I was happy to accept Augusto's invitation for a glass of wine. It was a month and a half since the grape harvest, and Augusto, like me, was preparing to rack the wine, draining it from one barrel to another and discarding the deposit. We decided, instead, to have some of his grappa. He pulled down two bottles from a high shelf. The liquid in the bottle he drank from was bright green, colored by two intact basil leaves that he had left to steep for some months. The grappa I chose, my favorite, was flavored by a thin slice of lemon peel and a sprig of sage.

Amelia Pichini

I continued only four doors down, as I saw that the door of Amelia's "club" was open, and I stepped inside. She greeted me with her friendly, wry smile, her head inquisitively tipped to one side. The club is a street-level room in her apartment, where she met on most days with some of her old friends. When I dropped in, she was preparing to leave Sorano, as she preferred the more temperate climate of the nearby seaside during the winter. I said my goodbyes and walked down to the piazza. I was passing by the town hall when Michele walked out with Albano, another of the Mari brothers. Michele somewhat embarrassedly thanked me from afar for his espresso, which I had paid for at the bar that morning. I heard Albano say something about the "americano," with a tart expression on his face as he rubbed his thumb and fingers together.

By then it was quite dark, and no one else was on the street except for Carlone, who emerged from the stairway that leads down to the old washhouse, struggling with a large, unwieldy object. I left him moaning and hobbling and made my way into the old town, past the church, and down to my house. I walked through the two apartments, the first of which had been the family home of the proprietor of the now closed Albergo Italia (Hotel Italy), and the second where Gino and his family used to live. Continuing out the back door and into the *via cieca* (cul-de-sac), where there are the entrances to my studio, my other small apartment, and the cantina, I went up and then down the cobblestoned street about thirty yards to Annetta's apartment.

Annetta is one of the few elderly townspeople, along with her sister Marietta, who chose to remain in their old homes. Annetta, six brothers and sisters, and her parents had all lived together in the 350-square-foot apartment where she now lives alone. Her place was full of family who had come for the funeral, so I made a quick exit. Before returning home, I looked up at one of Marietta's windows, where she would on dry days hang her few washed white articles. Some mornings, if she happened to be at the window, we would greet each other, and on those days when I would go to hang my own wash on the lines set up in the sunny area directly below the window, we would have a chat. That window looks directly into the *via cieca*, and I remember her peering from it, sometimes disapprovingly, when I worked messily outside one of the apartments.

Sparna in local dialect means a small terraced garden. *Sparne* are what once covered the far side of the river valley I see out my windows, and where the families of Sorano used to grow the produce they lived on. The landscape is now wild and overgrown, and only three or four sparne with olive or fruit trees or grapevines can still be discerned. The lane known as the Via della Sparna begins at the apartment where Annetta and Marietta were born and ends at the door to my home. Actually, the first entrance on the lane is to the cantina where Marietta and her husband, Sarino, made their wine.

Facing my door, to the right, buildings rise four or five stories, and most of the entrances on the lane are to ground-floor cantinas. To the left of the lane are the rooftop apartments of buildings that descend to the street below, the Via del Lato. On this very short lane, when Marietta was a teenager and Annetta a toddler, nine families lived with a total of thirty-seven children. Stairs lead up to Annetta's apartment, which is above another cantina that she now uses as a storage area. Opposite her house was a building that in 1982 was pulled down after a sustaining wall collapsed due to lack of normal maintenance. As no one was living in the building, which thirty years before had housed five families, the town's decision was to destroy it. A footbridge had led to two top-floor apartments. In one lived the Porri family of potters, including Luigino and his four siblings. In the other was Mariuccia with her husband and three sons. A small piazza was created in the place where the building once stood, and for many summers Willy Melcher, the first violinist of one of the world's premier string quartets, invited friends there to play chamber music.

Past Annetta's cantina, the next apartment on the right belonged to the Cerreti family of builders. Cerreti's granddaughter now comes on rare weekends from Florence. Just beyond the Cerreti place and up some steps is where Ciuccia and her son Cenciapane lived with their children and various other relations, all in one small room that is now abandoned. Below them was their cantina, which is now used to store wood, and opposite them lived the Savelli family with their two children. Under the Savellis' home is a tiny empty room where an uncle of the Savellis once lived. Proceeding down the *via cieca*, on the right is an abandoned cantina that belonged to Michele, the ex-Communist mayor. Up some more stairs, and above my cantina, lived the family of Matilde, who told me many stories about old Sorano. Matilde had married Silvano, one of the sons of Mariuccia, who was just up the lane. Next to my cantina was a manger where donkeys were stalled; it is now another room of my home.

On the other side of my "courtyard" is the apartment I bought from Leopoldo and the other members of the Mari family. Although the family lived down below my windows on the Via del Lato, they had used the previously inhabited apartment as storage for grain. The Mari family brood numbered more than ten, and they spent a lot of their time playing with other children at the end of the lane where I now live.

Gino, Sarino, and Maria Savelli were all born in the apartment I acquired from their sister Angiolina. The other brother, Sarino, became the husband of his close neighbor—the now deceased Marietta. Maria Savelli was Marietta's best friend, and they were born just a month apart in 1911. When she was eighteen, Maria was married off to a man from a nearby hamlet who had gone to America to seek his fortune. Maria was sent to join him in the United States, and had returned only once to Sorano in the 1950s.

Marietta and Maria kept in touch by writing and with the occasional phone call. Marietta told me that Maria would write about her onerous life in America and say how much she missed Sorano. Her husband, a truck driver, was often ill, and Maria had to work as a seamstress in a sweatshop until she was well into her sixties. A year before she died, Marietta asked me to find her sister-in-law in the Bronx in New York and take some gold chains for her grand-nephews. I also took pictures and tape-recorded greetings from Marietta, Matilde, and other old Sorano friends of Maria. Before I went to visit Maria I spoke with her daughter, with whom she lived. I was warned that Maria was old and forgetful, but I was welcome to come by and present the gifts. Maria, her daughter, and the daughter's husband lived together in a sad, dark apartment on Webster Avenue. When I first arrived, Maria was quite nervous and spoke haltingly in English. But once she saw the photographs and heard the tapes, her eyes lit up and we had an animated discussion in Italian about life as she remembered it in her hometown. Unfortunately, I did not have the opportunity to see Maria again, as she died only a few months later, shortly after her dear friend Marietta.

Back in Sorano, after Marietta's funeral I returned to my cantina, where Marietta, Maria, Matilde, Gino, Michele, Luigino, and Leopoldo had all gathered at one time or another. I sat at the round table I had made out of one of the ends of a large discarded wine barrel, and paused to drink a glass of wine to Marietta and all the others before returning to my winemaking tasks.

> In society no need is greater than that of gossip, the principal means
> of passing time that is one of the primary necessities of life.
>
> <div align="right"><i>PENSIERI</i> 8</div>

The changes of the past forty years have been particularly dramatic, and almost nothing in Sorano has proved to be immutable: not the walls, which fall due to neglect or have been changed from within to suit modern tastes; not the surrounding countryside or the inhabitants and their attitudes. One of the few things that have not changed is the most mundane. It makes Sorano like any other place and the soap operas *The Bold and the Beautiful* and *Santa Barbara* popular the world over: the fascination with scandals, problems, or even just ordinary goings-on elevated to a level of interest by rumor and innuendo, firing the imagination and keeping minds and tongues active.

In spending as much time as I have in Sorano, I became, as a matter of course, involved deeply in the town's more banal goings-on. I was the subject of gossip and I gossiped about others, which really was the only way to remain informed, inform others, and stay above the fray. But some incidents in one particular year thoroughly tarnished or perhaps simply cemented my already poor repute as an American.

Federico was, from when I first arrived in Sorano, always a good friend. He patiently helped me with learning Italian, and he introduced me to many of his friends. We often would visit his father's lovely vineyard and go on excursions together; he would even lend me his car if I needed to get building materials or other things for my home. For the first year that I was making wine, he helped, and became almost a permanent fixture at my place. Unfortunately, he fell in love with me. I tried to be tolerant for the sake of our friendship, and I did everything I could to convince him that I did not share his passion. As he seemed unable to prevent himself from hugging and kissing me in public places, even girlfriends of mine began to assume that something was going on between us. If I resorted to anger, it seemed only to increase his ardor.

One day, after yet another of the long and oft-repeated discussions about how I could not be his lover, we walked together up to the piazza. It was a weekend in the middle of the summer, so the piazza was full of people. I stopped at the Socialist bar, where many of my older friends were sitting outside playing cards, involved in animated games of *scopa* and *briscola*. Federico continued to walk up to his car, which was parked just outside the town hall, then turned and yelled with emotion at the top of his lungs, "*Chris, ti voglio bene.*" This seemed to indicate to me that he finally understood that we could be no more than friends. I responded in my, at the time, relatively rudimentary Italian: "Me, too. I wish you well." Or so I thought. As I went to walk in the bar, I noticed that everyone had stopped playing cards and was looking at me, some with astonished expressions on their faces.

Shortly thereafter, I was back again in the States for a brief trip and came across the movie *Marriage Italian Style* on TV. Sophia Loren and Marcello Mastroianni have an argument. She bursts into tears, crying out to the pastry chef played by Mastroianni, "*Ma Domenico, ti voglio bene.*" The subtitles read, "But Domenico, I love you."

Around this time my "Auntie" Annetta had taken under her wing a father-and-son pair from Venice who were looking to buy an apartment in the old town. They had already been in Sorano for some time and had made their mark. The father has a great fondness for wine and would spend most of his days up at the bars. The son is a recovering heroin addict who has frequent lapses, which had resulted in stolen and smashed cars, among other incidents. They had also become fast friends with Federico. These troubled fellows appealed to Annetta's motherly instinct, and she was keen to help them.

Matilde had been trying to sell her dark apartment directly above my cantina with its large window looking onto "my" courtyard for some time, and the two Venetians appeared to be interested in it. When I went to Annetta to express my reservations about having them on our little lane, she was irate. How dare I tell her who should and should not live in Sorano! This was her apartment to sell, and I must not interfere, she insisted. She was determined that they should have it, and two days later triumphantly told me that they were going to sign the agreement with Matilde soon. I knew Matilde quite well, having been introduced to her by Annetta, so I felt comfortable about going up to her apartment in the new town.

She was pleased to see me but confused when I said she should not rush into selling her apartment, because I knew somebody who might pay even more for it. (I did in fact know of someone from Naples who wanted a place in the town.) Matilde explained that the sale was out of her hands, and that I would have to speak to her son-in-law. Somewhat desperate, I went down to tell the story to Nadia, the Socialist bar-keeper, who usually comes through for me in a pinch. Massimo, she thought, knew the son-in-law, and indeed he did.

The situation was now getting a little out of hand. I knew that Massimo the Neofascist would love to undermine the Communist Annetta's plan, as they hold each other in great disdain. He made the call, and of course everything got back to Annetta. It had never occurred to me that she might be receiving a commission for her efforts, so not only did she think I was trying to supersede her authority as "Mayor" of our side of town, she also assumed that I was moving in on her cut of the deal. Perhaps worst of all was that I had asked Massimo of all people to make that phone call. Annetta was furious, and when she saw me she screamed that on that day she had lost her son. She did not speak to me for months thereafter.

Up in the piazza, where problems inevitably are either aired or resolved, I would see her some days with her old friends. If I were in earshot, I would hear her repeating in a rage, like a mantra, "*Lui e cattivo, cattivo, cattivo.*" He is wicked, wicked, wicked. In time, her anger subsided, and I am now back in my place at the head of the lunch table. And the Neapolitan bought the apartment.

I have not been only wicked with my acquired knack for gossip, storytelling, and exaggeration. I think I have also occasionally done good unto others. Walter is the town antiquarian. He came to Sorano about twenty years ago and managed to corner the antiques market in town. Walter has a goatee, which conceals somewhat the rolls under his chin, and he seems to be always amused by something or other. He is also a great salesman, having the ability to read his clients quickly, and he can effectively cajole, bully, or amuse them into buying almost anything. When I first arrived in Sorano, he had some beautiful tables, chests, and cabinets, mostly from the area and not for exorbitant prices. Since then the quality of his antiques has gone down and the prices have shot up. Now he has to go much farther afield, and brings things to his warehouse from the south of Italy, Romania, France, and England.

Some years ago I coveted a small ceramic bowl from the turn of the century with a simply painted rabbit bounding through flowers, in green, blue, yellow, and red. I pleaded with him to sell it to me for at least a year, but he preferred to continue to stub his cigarettes out in it. One day I found out what my last name is in Italian, so I decided to tell him as I passed his shop on my way up to the piazza. "*Conigliera?* (Rabbit warren?) *Non è vero.* (It can't be.)" He burst out laughing. I left him bent over, wheezing and gasping for air, and went up to do my day's shopping. We both suffer from asthma, so when I saw him constantly smoking and always going through this painful routine after laughing uproariously at a joke he had just told, it would disturb me.

On my way back down to the house, he came out of the shop and presented the bowl to me as a gift, but with the stipulation that my home be from that time known as "*Casa Conigliera.*" As it is quite like a warren, it seemed an appropriate name, and in time *La Conigliera* also became the name for my wine.

We had a mutual friend with a farm near Sorano, although she has since disappeared. Susan is half-English, half–Sri Lankan, and was the astrologer for *Tatler* magazine in London. She had read Walter's irises, or his palms, or had done his chart, and had determined that he has problems with his kidneys, which is true. He had been operated upon savagely a few years before for kidney stones, which had left him with a twenty-inch scar. She advised him that he must take good care to avoid a recurrence of his condition. The fact that she was able to guess this ailment was of profound consequence to Walter, who held her opinion in very high esteem after that. I was in London on a subsequent occasion, and told Walter that I had visited Susan there. I said that she had seen in her cards from afar that his lungs were in grave danger, and that if he did not stop smoking he would suffer and die from some horrible disease. Walter took this news very seriously and quit smoking on the spot. I did not tell him the truth for two years. He now breathes much more easily and occasionally rewards me with gifts and good prices on furniture.

Walter is also an ardent supporter of the Roma soccer club, and his enthusiasm is infectious. The other person responsible for my conversion to the Roman side is Debora, an Italian friend from the Open City who, when I facetiously suggested that I was for Roma's archrival, assaulted me in an unforgettable way. I immediately became a diehard fan of the team and her, and she continues to torture me to this day. *So also in love, that is the state of the soul that is the richest in pleasures and illusions, the best part, the surest route to pleasure and to a shadow of happiness, is pain.* (*Zibaldone* 142)

⌣

I have a variety of names in town, many of which are variations on my first name. "Cristoforo" is very unusual in Italian, despite the Christ-bearing saint and the Genovese explorer. I am called "*Cri*," "*Cricri*," "*Cristofo*," "*Critopo*," "*Cristofle*," or the cross-bearing "*Cristo*." For those who think I lead the good life, I am "*Bella Vita*." Some, who remember the 1954 film *Un americano a Roma*, in which the great comic actor Alberto Sordi continually repeats the nonsensical phrase "What's American, Boys," have taken to calling me "*Whats*." If the plethora of appellations causes confusion in others, I can be referred to quite simply as "*Cosa*." "*Ciao...uh...Cosa*." Hello, Thing (what's-your-name). More often than not, I am "*Americano*," "*America*," or "*Ame*" for short. In return I have assigned names to people in town, like "*Donnaiolo*" (ladies' man), "*Cavaliere*" (horseman) or "*Cacciatore*" (hunter). If there were a town mascot, *Cacciatore* would be the one. Whenever he sees me, even from across the piazza, he shouts out "*Americano!*" and gives a little wave of his hand. I yell back, "*Cacciatore!*" as he glances about him with a pleased expression to see if anyone has noticed our exchange.

Courses in ceramics, painting, and furniture restoration are held up in the fortress, appealing mostly to Italians during the August vacation. Cacciatore is always lurking around when the new students arrive, hoping to ingratiate himself with one of the ladies. He never had much success, however. One year, a pretty, blonde, long-legged American came roaring into town in a Maserati, and was dropped off by her tall, impeccably dressed Milanese boyfriend to take a ten-day course in painting. The cheerful Californian, with her broken Italian, became the talk of the town, and Cacciatore was the most persistent of her many admirers. At one point she came to ask me who the odd fellow was that was relentlessly following her around. I had made an ungracious assumption about her character, and I could not resist the temptation. "Cacciatore is," I said, "a count of considerable wealth who drives his little beat-up car and mingles with the townspeople because he wants to be treated as any ordinary person would be." Really? She bit, and for a couple of days Cacciatore had the time of his life and proudly became the envy of all the men in town. I think he still does not know about the little favor I did him.

I was always skeptical of Cacciatore's abilities as a hunter, despite his baying hounds, camouflage outfit, and ammunition belt. He dispelled any doubts when I had him come down to my house and from a window dispatch four annoying pigeons with four very quick, precise shots. As I retrieved the quarry, I was accosted by another sometime hunter, who angrily told me that it is illegal to use a gun in town and that he would denounce me to the authorities. I presented him with one of the pigeons, which he seemed to think was a suitable act of contrition. The other pigeons I dispensed to three of the local cats, which all regarded me with great suspicion and disbelief before they snatched up their unwieldy prizes and quickly waddled away.

Cacciatore was eager to know how I had prepared the birds. So as not to disappoint, I told him I had grilled them over coals in my fireplace. Despite my good intention, he was quite dismayed. I should have cooked them slowly in a covered pot with chopped vegetables, herbs, olive oil, and white wine. I continued my prevarication by telling him that they were in fact quite tough (*tosti*). He smiled and was satisfied, as I had proved his point. From that time forward, if our conversation gets beyond simple greetings, he almost invariably asks me, "*Come erano I piccioni?*" How were the pigeons? "*Tosti*," I reply, to his great amusement.

I have resorted to twisting the truth to titillate myself somewhat, but perhaps more to ingratiate myself with others. Some of the hardest capaccioli to crack in town have been those who have had little contact with foreigners and would prefer not to be bothered with them. Men tend to hunt, or feign interest in the pursuit and slaughter of anything from songbirds to wild boar. Unlike Cacciatore, those most devoted to blood sports are generally very gruff, expressionless if not scowling types that I have not even remotely managed to befriend.

At times I would wander down into the valley to explore some of the old *sparne* that families used to grow their food on. Slashing my way through the dense undergrowth, I discovered one abandoned terrace that was a typical morass of cane reeds, brambles, and old-man's beard—a fine nesting area for game birds, I had been told. When I saw the entrance to a partially collapsed cave, I moved forward and was startled by a very large, black, and hairy wild boar with protruding tusks that crashed away through the thicket. The original boar of the region had been reclusive and about the size of a medium dog. The type of boar I encountered is a crossbreed with the much larger Hungarian cousin. It was introduced to the area some thirty years ago, and there are more than a few stories of hunters being disemboweled by them. It was the end of January, and the hunting season was about to close. When I went back up to town, I told a few people about the boar, which I said was as big as a Fiat Cinquecento. Not even Cacciatore took my claim seriously.

A couple of days later, after a deluge with pelting rain, I returned to the valley. I crossed the ancient stone bridge, which the rushing, flooded river had practically submerged. As I came near to where I had seen the boar, I marveled to see that the heavy rain had revealed long-disused paths leading to some of the more inaccessible terraces I had never visited. Armed only with my old leaking Tuscan green canvas umbrella, I hacked and fell and slid my way along for hours. I discovered Bronze-Age caves and vast dry-stone walls that held up terraces and formed the foundations for the Castel Vecchio, a castle that was destroyed centuries ago. I found deep cisterns for collecting rainwater, and remnants of a canal system to take the water to the surrounding terraced gardens. The going was slow, and when I finally got back to town, it was well after dark. Rushing to do my shopping before the food shops closed at 7:00 p.m., I ran into Cacciatore. "*O! Americano. Come erano i piccioni? Ma…che cazzo hai fatto?*" What the fuck did you do? he asked. My shirt was torn by brambles, and I was soaking wet and covered in mud. "*Ho fatto la lotta con il cinghiale.*" I did battle with the boar, I lied. Amazed, Cacciatore took me into the Fascist bar and bought me a beer. There were other hunters present, and my mangled umbrella was held up as proof of my story. The following day a group of hunters went down to the valley and bagged three boars, one of which was bigger than any of them had seen in a long time. For the next several days, I was stopped in the street, clapped on the back, and bought coffee and glasses of wine by people I barely knew. My story was a great success.

I have sometimes cultivated appearances or even met challenges if only to contradict popular opinion or alter my reputation. I'm also not averse to doing good unto myself. As Michele said when I brought Swedish Pia to his wine cave, "What more do you want to know? About women? You have plenty of women down at your house, both beautiful and ugly. How many nationalities do you have hidden down there?" Over the years, many female friends have happily come to visit their friend in Tuscany. Drew from Los Angeles raised eyebrows when she went for long runs in tight shorts every day. Nowadays when I go cycling I often meet women joggers from town, but ten years ago the very notion of women exercising in public was almost scandalous. Michele made the mistake of making pointed remarks about the shapely derriere of my Rubenesque Belgian friend Stephanie, who easily understood the essence of his expressions. We were in the piazza, and she proceeded to berate me loudly in Flemish-inflected English, assuming that I was somehow in cahoots with the dirty old ex-mayor. Despite my efforts to placate her, she screamed louder and then burst into sobbing tears, much to the astonishment of all onlookers. Being Roman, Domitilla knew exactly what her actions would mean in a small Italian town. She took great glee in biting my neck or grabbing my ass in the bars and shops.

Shortly after the love declaration with Federico in the piazza, I was walking with the builder Massimo. We passed by the latest newcomer to flare the nostrils of the men of Sorano. Like the bombshell that changed Cacciatore's life forever, she was American, blonde, and taking a course in painting. But with her alabaster skin, tweezered eyebrows, aquiline nose, and divine proportions, she was a rare beauty. Doubting my masculinity, Massimo sneeringly said that I could not possibly get her into bed. I accepted his challenge, but without such salacious intent, and walked up to her as she sat on her stool sketching the Arco dei Ferrini—the medieval entrance to the town. She looked up at me witheringly but was relieved when I spoke more than two words of English and did not just stand and leer at her. She immediately accepted my invitation for a glass of wine, and we walked together, past the unbelieving Massimo, down to my house. We were not seen for the next couple of days, much to the fury of the single men in town. For some time thereafter, Cacciatore dispensed with our usual pleasantries. *"Numero Uno, sei tu!"* No, you are Number One, I would insist. In the end we always agree that I could only be the second best in town.

Another summer a group of Danes came to take a course on ceramics. The younger women tended to band together, likely fearing the wordless, drooling young men at the bars. One evening I invited all five to come with me to a hot spring in the middle of the countryside that empties into a series of three ancient Roman marble baths. As we walked up through the crowded piazza on that balmy summer's evening, we were followed by shouts of amusement, astonishment, and anger. The Americano was called by many names on that occasion, by those who could only imagine that we were off to an orgiastic bacchanal. We had a very pleasant time, lying in the smooth-worn baths, sipping wine, and regarding the near-full moon. I quite liked Birgitte, but she seemed not to be particularly interested in me. She later confided to me that her idea of a real man is Clint Eastwood.

The vast majority of people who visit in summer are Italian, but the few foreign women who come always elicit the most interest. Initially the young men in town eyed me as a potent adversary, but I now sit and explain that a little friendliness, subtlety, and a few words of English can go a long way. I have started to teach pithy expressions to some of the guys up at the bars. To those who can't master English, I write out snippets of Dante and Leopardi, Shakespeare and Pound, to recite or present to their lovely Italian girlfriends.

I say that the world is a league of villains against good men, and of those who are selfish against the benevolent. When two villains meet for the first time, they easily recognize each other, as though by a secret sign, for what they are; and immediately they are in agreement; or if their interests do not permit this, they are at least inclined to like each other and hold each other in great respect. If a villain has business dealings with another villain, he very often behaves honestly and does not cheat him; but if he is dealing with men of honor, he will surely be unfaithful to them and, if it suits him, will try to ruin them, even if they are brave men and able to avenge themselves. For he hopes, as almost always happens, to defeat their courage with his deceit.

PENSIERI I

There is a popular idea in town that Sorano is a *calamita*, pronounced with an accent on the *i*, which means "magnet." The town (actually it is said that there is a large lodestone in the nearby Monte Elmo) has certainly attracted an odd assortment of characters from around Italy and a few from the rest of the world, and these people are referred to as the *calamitati*. Malo, the brother of a world-famous film pornographer, cut just this type of eccentric figure for the few years that he was around. He always was impeccably dressed and, when he encountered anyone on his way to or from a bar—even my invariably sloppily attired self, covered in plaster dust from the work of renovation in my apartment—he would pause, doff his hat, slightly incline his head, and slur in Italian, as if he were addressing a most distinguished gentleman on the streets of his native Venice, "Good Day, Sir."

My fondest memory of Malo regards his beautiful companion, however, whom I surprised one day as I was working in my first apartment in town. While knocking the crumbling centuries-old plaster from my walls, I uncovered an interesting niche and pounded the volcanic tufo at its center with so much vigor that the block suddenly fell through into the next room, which happened to be Malo's bedroom in the adjacent apartment. I popped my head through the wall, and there she was in all her glory, standing with hands on hips. She let me have a good look for at least three or four seconds before scurrying out of the room.

Considering her marvelous attributes, I imagined that she could well have been one of Malo's brother's actresses. Malo, too, had some filmic aspirations, and knowing that I had experience with documentary filmmaking, he asked that I help him film the Easter procession in town one year. I demurred, but he did make the film, and I'm sure that he would have come back, perhaps with his brother, if he had known that I, a few years later, was to act in that same procession and be crucified as Christ, after having lugged the cross through the town streets. I fantasized that his companion would have been an exceptional Mary Magdalen.

As charming an idea as the *calamita* magnet is, I suggest, however, that Sorano is rather a *calamità*, with the accent on the final *a*, which means "calamity." Dante hearkened after an idealized Tuscan Florence that "abode in peace" within its ancient walls, "sober and chaste." He wrote in *Paradiso*, Canto XVI: "The mixture of peoples was ever the beginning of the city's ills."

One of the first outsiders to come to Sorano was a businessman from Bologna. He actually shares the name of a character whom Dante cast into one of the lowest circles of Hell for fraudulent counsel. This man has an apartment below one of mine. Unfortunately, all the property of my home is connected horizontally, passing through five different buildings. I have had problems associated with all the buildings, be they water leaks or roof or structural damage. Whenever there was a problem that I could resolve myself, like replacing a roof over one of my apartments, I did not ask anyone else in the building to pay their share. All the more fool me. Most repairs have been frought with complications and discord—particularly so with the Bolognese. He was the man who insisted that the floor in one of my apartments be redone, unnecessarily. Somehow I ended up doing the work of demolition, and then, when I was not around, he got the key from the builder and removed the old chestnut floorboards and most of the old floor tiles, which by right were mine. I never quite understood if the builder who put in the reinforced concrete beams and poured the floor was ever paid by the Bolognese, but I think it's far more likely that I was billed double. After a couple of episodes, I was reasonably prepared for his next ploy.

He arrived out of breath, sweating and a bit frantic, a cigarette dangling from his lips, with a builder from Parma. The builder's nickname, oddly, is that of one of Shakespeare's tragic heroes. For the sake of a disguise, and as he actually plays the part of a misguided dupe, an appropriate name for the builder would be Laertes, or Laerto, and the scheming Bolognese could aptly be called Claudio, "King of Denmark." The Bolognese does indeed have a somewhat kingly air, and a recently arrived Danish family has bought an apartment in Sorano—so allow me this conceit.

I had an encounter with Laerto's vitriolic side during the Gulf War, when he belligerently told me what he thought of Americans. But on this day he was all smiles and in a brightly colored Hawaiian shirt. It was, of course, a matter of urgency, so we went down to look at what was causing all the concern. There were cracks in the wall above Claudio's fireplace that extended to an important weight-bearing arched entrance to the room. It was plain to me that the blocks of tufo had been consumed by centuries of fires, and the wall had to be rebuilt. It is also likely that when the tons of sand-laden cement were poured to make the new floor, it may well have put considerable new stress on an already weakened wall. It was useless for me to say that his flue had done similar damage to my wall and that I had several years before done this same work without asking for payment from others. Not surprisingly, Laerto was immediately available to do the work.

The onus was put on me to accept the work, because, as they feverishly explained, if Laerto could not begin the next day, he would not be able to do the job at all. Otherwise, despite their claims, there really was no rush, but as it seemed to be a relatively simple intervention I decided not to fuss. There were, however, five other parties involved in the payment, so the story was somewhat more complicated. Nevertheless, the work was accomplished in two days, and I knew exactly what my fair share of the bill should be. I had requested a detailed estimate, which I did not receive until after the work was done. According to the bill, as prepared by Claudio, I was detailed to pay more than five times as much as I expected. Obviously I was paying for the whole job. Laerto almost immediately arrived at my door wanting his money. I simply paid him one-fifth and told him if he expected any more he could ask Claudio for it. He stormed away. Shortly thereafter I saw Claudio and told him what I had done, and that, further, I was still waiting, after six years, for the return of my chestnut boards and tiles, or cash equivalent. Claudio's cigarette dropped from his mouth.

The next day, I encountered Laerto in the piazza (of course). He walked up to me quite calmly and then suddenly became enraged. Claudio's plan had failed, and he was going to take it out on me, the hated American, who deserved to be ripped off because I have so much money—money I must have gotten by nefarious means. (Michele, the ex-mayor and my advisor on all things, including Italian/American relations, was being proved right yet again.) "*Tu sei uno stronzo, uno stronzo americano, veramente uno stronzo.*" You are a shit, an American shit, really a shit. I sighed, as I thought of other incidents not dissimilar to this one up in the piazza. Not only was I a shit, but also wicked, wicked, wicked and a shameless lover of the same sex. What did people think of me? "How could you come to Sorano and take advantage of these poor downtrodden people?" the Parmigiano went on. Laerto then backed up and hurled a very heavy twelve-inch-long old cast-iron key, striking me in the leg. At first I thought I was going to kill him, but I quickly came to my senses. If I was to kill somebody in the piazza, that would really be the end. I turned around and limped away.

In Dante's ordered Kingdom of the Lord his enemies are in Hell and his beloved in Heaven. My little mundane comedy has a hell, and I would not be displeased if the likes of Claudio and Laerto would go there. It has a heaven, but no Beatrice, and I am not sure anyone really deserves or can stay in paradise. The real world is an amalgam of the realms of Heaven, Purgatory, and Hell, although, on a scale, there is much more Heaven in Tuscan Sorano than in other places. The ideal, as Leopardi wrote, is to maintain equilibrium, "partly despised and partly respected." Heaven is transitory, if not wholly imaginary. Hell is a terrible situation that one can ideally escape from.

One of the curiosities of our contemporary world is that with education and the spreading of wealth, people now have the ability to advance themselves from one realm or one circle to the next. The problem as Leopardi saw it is that once you have achieved a pleasure, you can no longer be satisfied by it. For a generation that has lived through a war, or simply moved on from their homes in the old town of Sorano and attained some degree of prosperity, it must be distressing to see their sons and daughters chronically dissatisfied. So, if one digs deeply enough, one finds that many of Sorano's old people look back almost rosily at their past way of life. Nevertheless, as in any society, there always were misanthropes, feuds, injustice, and deceit. In the real world, even Heaven has its "calmaties."

One deduces the usual consequences of the superiority of the ancients over the moderns in order of happiness. Imagination is the primary fount of human happiness. The more this reigns in man, the more he will be happy. We see it in children. But this cannot reign without ignorance, at least a certain ignorance like those of the ancients.

ZIBALDONE 168

Just as Dante looked to a time that was free from "the entanglements of the deceitful world, the love of which corrupts many souls,"[6] Leopardi lionized a Homeric world in which the ancients, poets, children, the ignorant, and the uneducated "abound" in "beautiful air" and indefinite ideas. "Ignorance which alone can hide the confines of things is the principal font of indefinite ideas. Thus it is the major source of happiness."[7] The reality of these "ideal" worlds is that of Sorano's past, in which a privileged few lorded it over the ignorant masses, who had no rights and lived in squalid, cramped, disease-plagued, vermin-infested quarters—conditions similar to those of the hundreds of millions of desperate poor in today's developing world. The process of civilization may have unfortunate consequences and may spread the deceit and barbarity of the city, but modernization has brought education, cures for diseases, and reasonable living conditions. The changes to Sorano have been abrupt and sometimes ugly, but embracing Dante's and Leopardi's romantic ideals could lead to the demand to expel immigrants, or, by extension, could be used by apologists for governments that do nothing for their poor and downtrodden.

---

[6] Dante Alighieri, *Paradiso* Canto XV
[7] Giacomo Leopardi, *Zibaldone* 1464–65

A house hanging in the air, suspended by ropes to a star.

ZIBALDONE 256

Laura, a young woman from Sorano, was so taken with my exhibition of photographs of the far side of town and my painted room that she went away with two prints that now hang on her walls. Other people were impressed enough with my work that they, too, began to paint their rooms in the traditional way, and it has now become something of a fad to do so. So I was somewhat baffled when Laura came to visit the house again a couple of years later, and said, "Oh, so you have painted your house like Moreno."

After I proved that I could make rather good wine, some younger people from the new town, and some of the outsiders who had moved to Sorano, like the Florentine Giuliano, cleaned up three or four of the cantinas in the old town and started to make wine, too, with varying degrees of success. If the Americano could do it, anyone could. Gianni, a Jew from Rome who bought and renovated his house in the ghetto, the old Jewish quarter of Sorano, stopped by for a glass of wine. His comment was, "Hmm. Excellent. It is good that you decided to make wine like Giuliano."

Not long ago an old friend who had once lived in Sorano came by to see my house, now that it is essentially finished. We walked through all the rooms, and I explained how and where I had replaced floors, knocked down and rebuilt walls. He could not believe that I had redesigned and constructed two of the fireplaces and made them look old and original. He admired the old light switches and the silk-wound electrical wiring. I showed him all the furniture I had either designed or restored. He was amused by the old stove I had found by a roadside and the refrigerator that had been thrown out in town, both of which were from the fifties and took quite a lot of work to get going again. He was touched to see that I had Marietta's lovely old wood-burning stove, which she had been given shortly after she was married. We then walked into the cantina that he remembered coming to with Ermanno in his youth. The cantina had changed so little, he remarked, but my wine was better than the one they used to make. As he left, he shook my hand and said that all the hard work had paid off. He said that despite remembering those who had lived in the apartments before me, he felt strongly that this was now my home, and he felt well in it.

My closest ties have proven to be with Sorano's oldest inhabitants. Of those whom I interviewed, four have died. Gino is now bedridden, having lost his leg to gangrene, the same infection that took his father's life in 1929. Uncle Carlo, who taught me winemaking, is very ill with leukemia. As each person goes, I feel my moorings slip. Once Annetta, Michele, Leopoldo, Luigino, and Ivana are no longer here, their houses abandoned or sold to new arrivals, I may no longer be at home.

> Looking ahead,
> The bewildered traveler vainly searches for goal or reason
> On the long road which lies before him,
> And sees that he has now become
> A stranger here where dwells the human race.
>
> "THE SETTING OF THE MOON" (1837)

SORANO 1998

Melancholy, when feigned, can be pleasing for a short time, especially to women. But when it is genuine, it is to be avoided by the whole human race, and in the long run nothing but cheerfulness pleases in society, or brings good fortune with it. For in the end the world wishes rather to laugh than to weep, and it is not wrong.

PENSIERI XXXIV

When Leopardi was spurned by one of the women he loved, Fanny Targioni Tozzetti, he penned one of his bleakest poems, *"A Se Stesso"* ("To Himself"), and contemplated death. He also wrote, "I do not ask for what the world calls gifts; not for riches nor love, the only thing worth living for. I ask for what is considered the greatest of evils, death. I've had enough, enough of life."[8] When a vivacious and enchanting Roman girlfriend rejected me, I became quite bitter about most things and contemplated leaving Italy. But another year has passed, and things are beginning to look up. Uncle Carlo's leukemia is in remission, and he is working in his vineyard and cantina with renewed vigor. He has started to make an excellent sparkling white wine that he calls "Pum." I took two bottles to a New Millennium's Eve celebration in Manhattan, and the Pum compared favorably to the Dom Perignon. Gino is now in an electric wheelchair that permits him slowly to go via the main road to Bar Dancing. The rest of the way down to the piazza is too steep, so Gino's old friends come up to share a bottle of wine with him. Nearing a century of age, Maria is still going strong behind the bar. Her daughter helps her on some days, and her grandson makes the potent red wine. Maria's husband was known as "Gigo," a diminutive, familiar form of the name Guido. As was often the case, the wife was called by the feminine version of the husband's nickname, and so she became "La Giga." *Giga* happens to mean "jig" in Italian, which suggested the name for the bar.

Most of my old friends made it through the winter, although

---

[8] *from the posthumously published poetic fragment, "The Hymn to Ahriman."*

some not easily. Michele went to hospital with pneumonia, and both Leopoldo and Luigino suffered heart failure. Nevertheless, Luigino is already back working at his potter's wheel, and Michele and Leopoldo are playing cards and debating up at the Berlusconi bar. In the meantime I made a great leap forward. Heating is necessary six months of the year in Sorano. For twelve years I barely warmed my increasingly large home with wood-burning stoves. In the past, when there were ten people to a small apartment, four to a bed, and the fire was kept going in the grate all day long, a reasonable temperature could be maintained even during the coldest days of winter. Still, the collecting of wood and transportating it to the homes in the old town was difficult, and nowadays it is very costly compared to other fuel sources. Despite global warming, the tramontana wind still blows bitter cold. It grew a bit tiresome waking up in the morning in my smoky bedroom, under a mountain of blankets, with a wool hat, a cold hot-water bottle, and the bedside thermometer reading 45 degrees Fahrenheit.

With the renovations essentially done, I no longer could do manual labor to keep myself warm. If ever I went on a trip for a day or two, I would come back to a refrigerator for a house, and it would take a week to heat up the thick walls if I was away for an extended period of time. To maximize the heat production of the stoves, I ran the old-style sections of white enamel–painted stovepipe as far as I could, even through rooms that had no stoves. The many curves and long piping resulted in the pipe joins malevolently leaking smoke and dripping black creosote. If I wanted to heat my whole place, I had to stoke up all three inefficient and aged stoves, but whenever I used more than one at a time, they would smoke badly. When the wind swirled, or blew at just the right egregious angle, the stovetops would spew palls of smoke. Much of the time, windows had to be cracked open to provide enough air for the stoves to pull properly, and often doors and windows had to be left wide open to clear the smoke out. On my rare trips to Rome or Florence, people would be repulsed by the barbarian American who reeked of garlic and wood smoke.

Even though I had always sworn that I would try to be true to tradition, would avoid certain accoutrements of our modern world, and do all I could to minimize my own personal impact on the environment, I decided, with the dollar at an unprecedented high against the lira, to put in an oil-fired heating system with radiators in every room. The job was, as I have grown to expect, long and chaotic. I had to pull up sections of floor, drill and pound holes through the three-foot walls, and chip out tracks in the plaster for the copper piping. Just trying to match the seven old colored-lime mixes, to paint over the various patches, took an inordinate amount of time. I was reminded of the months, indeed years, of working on my place while living in it: the pervasive, clinging smells of cement, sand, plaster, and tufo dust; the gritty film that covered tabletops, drinking glasses, and pillowcases; the sensation of being permanently filthy. But ultimately the change has been revelatory. I am now comfortable in my home during the cold months. I don't have to wear long johns, a coat, and a hat when I work at my desk, and my clothes no longer stink of smoke. I have a greater appreciation for why people left their homes in the old town in the early 1960s. Until they became accustomed to the central heating, as well as the running water and the electricity to power more than just two light bulbs, it must have seemed like heaven.

I have left the stoves and most of the stovepipes in place, so I can still perfectly roast a pheasant over several hours in Marietta's *cucina economica*, or fire up a smoky stove to make my place redolent of times past. But now, when I come from afar, all I have to do is ask Ivana to push a button a couple of days before I arrive and I return to find my home warm, dry, and welcoming.

While installing the central heating, I was also busy acquiring two of the *sparne* in the hills of the valley opposite town. The long-abandoned, wildly overgrown terraces made up a plot of land that is marked as the *cocceria* (pottery) on the local ordnance survey map. On the narrow strips of land there are five caves, some likely dating to the Bronze Age, dug from a cliff of tufo that drops fifty feet from other terraces above. One of the caves was used as a pottery prior to the twentieth century, and another was a habitation with a large fireplace. I may yet become a troglodyte, as were the Etruscans and the Villanovan people that preceded them. Regressing in the countryside as I modernize in town.

I discovered the cocceria during a walk in the valley. I had followed one of the *vie cave etrusche*—paths that were cut out of the sheer hillside by the Etruscans well over two thousand years ago—that lead up to the plains surrounding Sorano. In places the walls of the paths rise up thirty feet or higher, forming a winding man-made cavern. Ancient chisel marks are still apparent but begin at about shoulder height, indicating the erosive effects of weather and heavy traffic over so many centuries. Nowadays along these Etruscan paths I encounter boars more often than people.

Three paths branch away from the closest bridge to town. The first proceeds east along the river, passing a few vegetable gardens at the water's edge. That path, although lost in some places, leads to a formerly popular frigid water hole, and finally, after a few kilometers, to the river's source. The second path goes west along the river and through the open valley, until it further branches in other directions, meandering to the hidden ruins of a monks' cloister or passing through a sylvan glade of high shade trees before entering one of the narrow, dark, high-walled Etruscan pathways. The path I chose makes a quick, steep ascent from the river, soon coming to two large caves. In one cave Sergio keeps his tractor—and in bad weather his horse. In the other cave, which is enormous, Massimo has a small chicken coop, but most of it is crammed full with the doors, windows, sinks, toilets, and tiles he has collected over the forty years he has been working as a builder.

Continuing along, to the right Massimo's fallow field has been taken over by hip-high ferns. To the left the hill rises sharply and sometimes spills onto the path where the old dry walls have crumbled and fallen. Smaller trails, some barely identifiable, cut up the hillside to the entrances of individual terraces. Unaccustomed to passersby, Massimo's large dog lunged at the gate to his penned-in area, barking frantically long after I had gone. The next field was a vineyard last tended by Mario. Weeds now choke the once neat rows, and the vines are either dead or straggly and no longer producing fruit. Mario was a much beloved *personaggio* of Sorano who died of cirrhosis in 1989. Unable to understand him at the time because of my rudimentary Italian, I remember him thin and jaundiced, lying on a cot in his "club," animatedly holding court to an enthralled group of friends. I bought his storeroom from his brother Leopoldo and other relatives, and made it into my first little apartment.

Opposite the entrance to Mario's field is a trail that is easily followed, as it is almost daily trod by a couple of old men from the town. Elidio has his garden, and at the end Michele, the ex-mayor, has his vineyard. It is possible, with a sharp machete, to go beyond and up above Michele's vineyard to the top of the hill, where there are ruins of Castel Vecchio. On this occasion, I had just passed the upright pillars that remain of the previously arched entrance to the "Old Castle," and I noticed a couple of steps that disappeared into a thicket. Chopping my way, I found eighteen steps that make up an enchanting narrow winding stairway, carved out of the tufo, leading down to the terraces of the cocceria.

The collapsed entrance to the abandoned pottery is just to the right of the bottom of the stairway, and the openings to the other caves are along the 150-foot-long cliff wall. Two of the caves have weathered wooden doors, and one has a white 38 stenciled above it, a civic number indicating that it was registered at one time as taxable property in the town hall. Long branches of holm oak, maple, and black locust hung down the cliff face, providing some relief from the blazing sun that bakes the south-facing plot. Wading through the dry golden grass, I was surprised to find late in August some remaining small but tasty peaches and plums hanging from the neglected fruit trees.

Three huge boulders of tufo, fallen from above during a long-ago landslide, lie about the two terraces. One of the boulders forms the end of a dry wall that runs the length of the upper terrace. The wall was in a sad state of disrepair, having been invaded by the destructive roots of a large fig, old-man's beard, and brambles, but the fig was covered in fruit, and even the brambles bore sweet blackberries. Hidden among the weeds, on the top of the wall, I found vines, some with a few dry, ambrosial grapes. The vines had once been trained onto a pergola, the old wooden poles lying scattered and broken on the ground below.

The upper terrace affords an almost intimate view of bowl-shaped Sorano, being on an opposite hill at about the same altitude as the town and just close enough to hear Annetta chattering from her window to someone in the street. The lower terrace was protected from peering townspeople by closely spaced and tall black locusts, planted to prevent erosion on the steep bank that drops down to the Etruscan path below.

At the far end of the terrace was a battered old gate. The wood was rotten and broken off in places, but the gate was thoroughly intertwined with creepers and I did not try to force it open. The vegetation was so dense I could not see what lay beyond. Turning back and looking onto the two terraces of the cocceria, I realized with pleasure where all my next considerable efforts might be devoted.

I learned that a woman from Lecco, in northern Italy, owned the cocceria. Her family left Sorano in the 1930s, although they returned frequently thereafter to visit their hometown. Signora Franca inherited the plot upon her mother's death, and since the 1950s had rented it to a lady in town who used it to make a vegetable garden, and for some years let Gino's son Graziano keep his horse in one of the caves. However, for ten years the garden had lain unused, and it seemed that Franca wanted finally to sell it. I spoke to her by phone, but after several months she confessed that her son was reluctant to part with the land. As a youngster he had spent summers in Sorano and was justifiably eager, despite the sale of the family's home, to maintain some tie to his ancestral town.

With a fellowship from the Soros Foundation, he had just completed a degree course in economics at the Central European University in Budapest. He met his American girlfriend there, and they had returned together to Lecco. He was seeking employment and was hoping to get a job closer to Sorano, buy an apartment in town, and do the gardening on the weekends. I explained to him that it would be a tremendous amount of work to get the cocceria back in shape, and that if it were allowed to go any more wild it might not be worth the effort, but he was not to be swayed. Knowing that he had not seen the state of the land, and that he had no idea how expensive apartments had become in town, I still held out some hope. He came to Sorano while I was away in August, and I was not unduly surprised to get an e-mail from him informing me that he was reconsidering my offer.

After completing the deed I immediately got to work. With great clumsy zeal I started by scything the upper terrace, but fortunately someone lent me a gas-powered strimmer and I found it to be much more efficient for cutting the very long grass. I had to stop and dig up nettles with their remarkably extensive root systems, and there were also little black locust seedlings, attached by very large roots to a parent tree.

After a few days' digging those and other weeds up, the ground looked like a moonscape. I knocked down the gate at the far end of the lower terrace and attacked with a *ronca* (a large curved blade attached to a long handle) the jungle of cane reed and brambles that had begun to invade that corner. I also opened up what was the principal entrance to the cocceria, clearing out the wide slope bounded by two other overrun dry walls, and the small trail that comes directly up from the Etruscan path.

Even in the middle of October the heat was intense, and I easily would go through three liters of drinking water a day. Sometimes I would seek shelter from the sun in one of the caves. The cave that likely was a home in the not-distant past is about three hundred square feet—almost as big as one of my apartments in town. Like the Etruscan paths and the rest of the caves on the plot, it had been hollowed out of the tufo by hammer, chisel, and pickax. Not done with particular care, the cave is irregular in its widths and heights, and the raw ten-foot-high ceiling and walls are patterned by mostly irregular chisel and chop marks. The original entrance is a large half-oval that at some time was closed off with blocks of tufo, leaving the space for the door and two windows on hinges set above the lintel. To the right of the door is a large fireplace, of the type found in farmhouses all around the Sorano area. It has a very worn, unfinished tufo-block base, a plaster hood, and a plank for a mantle. A large hole at the back of the fireplace very effectively draws the smoke outside. Running the full width of the other side of the room is a recently built feeding trough where Graziano's horse ate his hay and oats.

Sixty years ago, when families still relied upon the produce they grew in their gardens, the terraces were all well maintained. Old-man's beard, brambles, and nettles were not permitted to get a foothold. *Canapa*, or hemp, was used for making bed linen and clothes. It was so ubiquitous that my terraces are often referred to by people in town as a *canapaio*. Despite this, I have yet to find a hemp plant. The very tall cane reeds, similar looking to bamboo, were cultivated for making boxes and supports for the vineyards, or were just dried and used for starting fires. As in my cave, they were even used in constructing the armature for fireplace hoods. They continue to be prized for making woodwind reeds. They were grown carefully, because they are very invasive: Today they are all over the hills, and the rhizomes are very hard to dig up and eradicate from a field.

If they were allowed to grow at all, holm oaks and figs, with extensive roots damaging to walls, were severely pruned. The now big uncared-for trees have sunk their roots deep into the tufo, opening cracks and causing several landslides in the valley in recent years. The front of the old pottery collapsed because of this problem, and there are cracks also in the cliff above my other caves. Therefore, I realized, despite the agreeableness of the shady limbs, I was going to have to cut down the trees at the edge of the terraces above mine.

Elidio was using a small portion of the plot above for a vegetable garden. Although he liked to give the impression that he was the *padrone*, I knew that the real owner was Alessandra, an old lady in town. Alessandra was the woman who had rented the cocceria for forty years from Signora Franca before it was sold to me, and Elidio happened to be the last person to cultivate a garden there, before he moved above. Then, as now, in exchange for using Alessandra's land he gives her half of the vegetables.

Elidio had also made an extraordinary fence all around the perimeter of my plot, to keep porcupines and boars from digging up his potatoes. He must have gone to a garbage dump and gathered just about everything to make his *pezzo di resistenza*. More than anything else, he used the flat heat-exchange piping from the back of refrigerators, but there also were panes of glass, mirrors, doors, windows, corrugated iron, green plastic roofing, and lots of bits and pieces of wood and metal—all bound together with wire and string. In one corner of the garden he just piled shoes and tied them to upright wooden sticks. This work indicated either his impecuniousness or the mind-set of a generation that wastes nothing. Although the barrier served its purpose, it was very unattractive, and I have saved only a portion of it as an example of Tuscan ingenuity.

When I first started to work on the cocceria, Elidio appeared one afternoon and we walked together around the terraces. He helpfully identified each of the fruit trees and gave me some tips about how to prune them. I mentioned that I was planning to cut down some of the trees above the cliff. He agreed that it was necessary and responded with a noncommittal, "Si, si, vediamo." Yes, we'll see.

Some of the trees had sprouted well down the cliff face, so I needed someone to assist me with the rather precarious job. One Sunday I arranged for Roberto, a fearless and acrobatic local woodsman, to come with his ropes and chainsaws. We got to work early, and by mid-morning we had done much of the cutting, being very careful to remove only what posed a danger. Unfortunately, Roberto slipped and hurt his knee, leaving me to do the bulk of the work alone. I set about stripping the cut limbs of their smaller branches, twigs, and leaves. I left some of the black locust poles intact to use as posts in the future, and cut up the oak and maple. By mid-afternoon I had made a vast pile of debris, and I set it alight. The fire burned hot and high, and I stood by with my pitchfork to keep it under control.

All of a sudden I heard someone yelling, *"Butti l'acqua sul fuoco!"* Throw water on the fire! Put it out! I was startled, unable to think what the problem could possibly be. As it was past October 15, I could legally have a bonfire, and the fire did not appear to have spread. I could not tell where the yelling had come from until I looked up and saw Elidio standing at the top of the cliff. *"Butti l'acqua sul fuoco,"* he screamed again, his voice echoing in the valley. I had no water, so the idea was absurd. Elidio came charging down the stairway. He continued to yell, beside himself with rage. "How dare you come here, Americano, cutting the wood without permission, acting as though you own the place! This is my land and you have stolen that wood."

He was berserk, this gentle quiet man, and I had somehow provoked him. Whatever I said only made him angrier. He was particularly upset about one oak that he had planned to cut for firewood. It was, in fact, rather small and at the very edge of the precipice. As the agile Roberto was barely able to get to it, the eighty-year-old likely would have killed himself if he had tried. I told him to take the pieces of oak away. "You are an American shit—go back where you came from and leave us alone!" I spread the fire and put it out with some difficulty, and then I walked away, leaving him glaring at me with hatred. I walked down to the valley and back up to town, wondering how such a confrontation could have happened yet again. Do these people really think Americans are so despicable, or is it something about my own character that sets them off?

I went straight to Alessandra's apartment and rang the bell. She was having her siesta but was happy to see me nonetheless. A few years before, she had admired some cascading violet petunias I had in a pot outside one of my windows. She asked me where she might be able to get such a beautiful plant, so I went and bought one for her and had presented one to her as a gift every year since. On this occasion I walked into her kitchen and apologized for stinking of smoke and being so filthy and sweaty. I contritely told her about what had transpired with her friend Elidio. I explained that I knew she was the owner of the land above mine, but I had not wanted to trouble her with the matter. Further, I pointed out that I could have notified the town hall of the dangerous situation and required her to have the trees cut down. In fact, it had cost me quite a lot to hire Roberto.

She was surprised that Elidio had claimed to be the owner, and she told me that I was free to do whatever I wanted. I thanked her and stood up to go. But, she added, there was another issue that was troubling her. She had heard that I had bought the cocceria, and she was quite upset about it. She claimed that back in the 1950s she had put a down payment on the land of 50,000 lire (worth about twenty dollars in the year 2000). She had not been able to pay for the deed, and so in the end had decided not to buy it. "Signora Franca sold the land to you and did not even reimburse me my down payment," she said, frowning. So, with great American munificence, I pulled my wallet out of my back pocket and presented her with a 50,000 lire note, which seemed to please her well. I thanked her again and went on my way.

I marched straight down to the valley and up again to the cocceria. I raked the fire back together and relit it. Soon enough, there was Elidio at the cliff edge screeching hoarsely, "*Butti l'acqua sul fuoco.*" He went on another screaming tirade. The second he paused, I yelled up at him: "It is not as though you are the owner to tell me to stop burning this fire." Silence. "Well, who is the owner?" "Alessandra." Silence. "She did not give you permission to make this mess." "Yes, she did." (She had done so only ten minutes before.) "*Bugiardo!* Liar! She would have told me if she had." After the long string of abuse, I was thoroughly fed up, so I yelled back up at him to "*va fa un culo,*" and he disappeared.

The next day, of course, several people who had heard the hysterical screaming in the valley stopped me to ask what on earth I had done to make Elidio so furious. I had to repeat my version of the events at least five times. Fortunately I found Luigino's sympathetic ear. He was very interested to hear how things were progressing at the cocceria, and he suggested he might come and pay a visit later in the week.

Later that afternoon I was walking back down from the piazza after a coffee at one of the bars. Standing in the street outside her apartment were Alessandra and Elidio. She was angry, and proclaimed that as Elidio was cultivating the garden on her plot, he could be considered the *padrone*. With puffed chest Elidio loudly accused me of having cut down everything forty feet into Alessandra's plot. His claim was decidedly exaggerated, as I had cut only up to the edge of the cliff. Michele, the ex-mayor, came ambling along and was more than happy to adjudicate. He said that the law states that I can cut only as far up the cliff as my curve-bladed *ronca* would reach—about fifteen feet. I testily explained that the trees were a danger and that I could have required Alessandra to have them cut. Michele refused to listen to my protests, and decided that I had to give all the wood to the beaming Elidio. So, over the next few days, I carried the cut limbs and branches up the stairway and deposited them outside Elidio's garden.

I don't know why Michele took Elidio's side, but apparently he felt a bit badly about it. A few days later, he said that he had arranged for a mutual friend of ours, Eliseo, to give me the plot of land next to mine. The plot Michele was speaking of happened to be the jungle beyond the main entrance to the cocceria, where, I later realized, I had my encounter with the enormous boar. Eliseo had no use for it and was happy that I would take it on. As a result of the trouble with Elidio, I got another piece of land as big as the two terraces of the cocceria.

The previous week there had been a tempest with very strong winds, which knocked over the top of one of my chimneys. I spent most of the day after the bonfire incident on the roof rebuilding the chimney. At one point Don Enzo, the town padre, called to me from the windows of the rectory, two stories above where I was working. Don Enzo speaks with a booming *basso profondo*, yet he chooses to use a large microphone attached to his chest at Mass. "*Cristoforo* (he is the only one in town to get my name right in Italian), *che cosa' hai fatto ad Elidio?*" Elidio is such a humble, unassuming, churchgoing, God-fearing man, who goes up to visit the grave of his dear departed wife every day. What did you do to make him so angry? Standing on the peak of my roof I explained to him that unfortunately I had been involved in a number of disputes of this type with the *capaccioli* (hardheads) of Sorano. They can seem to be nice and caring, their brows untroubled, and then the next minute screw their faces up frighteningly and spit venom. Don Enzo appreciated this explanation, as he, too, had come from outside Sorano. In his fifty years here he had many of his own run-ins with *capacciolo* madness. Knowing that I am a photographer, he playfully proposed that I do a show illustrating a few of the characters from town when they are calm, juxtaposed to photos of them angry. I responded that even if I could get them to distort their faces with fury, it probably would not be in my best interest. I suggested that, instead, I do a show entitled simply "*Capaccioli Tranquilli.*"

A few days later, Luigino came to the cocceria as I was finishing clearing the three boulders of the brambles and ivy that had totally enveloped them. I was delighted to find that the boulder at the end of the dry wall had been hollowed out to make a large oven for baking bread and pizza. The mouth of the oven at the center of the rough boulder was finished with brick, stacked on either side, with an arch above. At the back of another boulder I uncovered four steps going up to the leveled top, with a raised border around the edge. Luigino agreed that this must have been where some of the pots were laid to dry. We walked together to the cave that had been the pottery, last used by his great-uncle Lorenzo Porri. The pottery was abandoned when Lorenzo died at the end of the nineteenth century. We clambered over the large pieces of tufo that had collapsed from the front of the cave and were partially blocking the entrance. There is one large room, with two smaller cells off to the side. Because of the layout of the cave and the fact that the floor is several feet lower than the ground outside, it might well originally have been made as a tomb. Luigino pointed out the ceiling blackened by the wood-burning kilns. There were no remnants of the kiln for firing pots, but we did find signs of the smaller kiln that heated lead, copper, and other metals used in the preparation of glazes, and the recess in a wall where the glazes were mixed.

Before he left, Luigino peered into the cave with the fireplace. This, he said *sotto voce*, was the *Grotta della Topa*. *Topa* in Tuscan Italian is a crude term for a woman's genitals. "The Pussy Cave?" I repeated incredulously. "You don't mean to say that this was a *bordello*?" Luigino pointed out that the cocceria is the only plot of land in the valley with two entrances, convenient for a quick escape. He had only heard tell of the woman, nicknamed "Topa," who lived in the cave after his great-uncle had given up the pottery. By the time he was a young boy in the 1920s, she was no longer there. Presumably Topa lived in and worked from the cave roughly between 1900 and 1920. Enthralled with the knowledge that my small bit of land not only was the pottery but also the whorehouse of the town, I went to seek out some of my old friends to see if they knew anything more about Topa.

There is no disputing that the cave was a habitation. Prior to homes being built with blocks of tufo, people in the area were troglodytes. In a town near Sorano, several families were living in caves well into the twentieth century. The Etruscan path below the cocceria was one of the three principal routes leading to Sorano before the present roads were constructed in the 1930s. The name of the path was the Via della Cavarella. Michele and Luigino remember that when they were children, in addition to the gardens and pottery, there was also a carpenter, and other artisans worked out of the caves and terraces that lie alongside the path. Because of the stenciled 38 outside the Grotta della Topa, I went up to the archivist in the town hall, to see if he had any records pertaining to 38 Via della Cavarella. The information in the numerous large leather-bound tomes is incomplete and often illegible. For example, the date of birth of Luigino's great-uncle Lorenzo Porri was noted as July 8, 1837, but there was no date of death. Unfortunately, there also was no information on number 38. Likewise, no one other than Luigino could recall anything about the Topa of the Grotta della Topa, but I suspect that this forgetfulness may be due to some old-fashioned sense of *gentilezza*.

As it happens, there may have been another Topa. Her name, I discovered, was Annunziata Borsetti, and she was born in 1886. The accepted story is that she was married to Antonio Borsetti, whose nickname was "Rat"—*Topo* in Italian. Like La Giga, La Topa was named after her husband. In the more controversial telling, however, Topa, after she had resigned from her "oldest profession," married one of her clients, and by extension he became rightly known as the Italian masculine gender version—the corresponding male member—to herself. I will stay, nevertheless, with the polite version of the tale.

During the summer of 1990 I was living and working in my first apartment. The concrete floor had recently been poured, and I had knocked all the plaster off the walls and begun to repoint between the blocks of tufo. A dangerous area of bulging wall, through which the Bolognese Claudio's chimney passed, had to be taken down and rebuilt with new blocks of tufo and brick. The only order in the room was in one corner where I collected and laid out pieces of the centuries-old plaster that I had scraped to reveal the twenty or so layers of lime, giving me ideas for the colors I was eventually to paint the room. The rest of the room was an infernal mess of piles of dusty plaster, broken sooty pieces of old tufo, stacks of new tufo blocks, sand, and bags of cement and lime. A forest of jack posts, locally called *cristi* as they resemble crucifixes, held up the beams of the ceiling.

The previous September I went to the famous once-yearly antiques fair in Arezzo, which draws dealers from all over Italy. There I bought a small but very lovely fifteenth-century simple wrought-iron bed, which I had placed in the center of the room. A plastic tarp did little to keep the grime and dust away from my sheets, but exhaustion and copious amounts of wine tended to make me immune to the filth. In the middle of one night I awoke to squeaking noises and looked up to see two large rats hanging from the iron loops of the bedhead, illuminated by the light of a crescent moon perfectly framed in one of the windows. I jumped up, and they skittered away, hiding themselves in the rubble. Tired and sozzled, I returned to bed, hoping the rats would leave me in peace.

Some time later, I was again startled awake, but this time by two small, fleshy objects squirming on my chest. I grabbed them and flung them across the by-then moonlight-less pitch-dark room. Without electricity, I reached for my candle but could not light it as my lighter had run out of fuel. By the flashes of the repeatedly struck flint I could find no signs of the intruders. After a long while, I lay back on the bed, and again fell deeply asleep. The next time I woke up, I found the rats rooting around in the bed with me. I turned the bed out, but they kept coming back. Eventually I just gave up and went to sleep on the curb outside the apartment.

The next day I was able to understand that the fearless rats thought they had found a nice warm place to nest their newborn babies. After the babies abruptly disappeared, the rats repeatedly returned to the bed to search for them. I related my flesh-crawling tale up at one of the bars, and I was quickly dubbed "Topo," the first of my nicknames in Sorano. Someone clever then started to call me Critopo, which stuck for quite a long time.

Because of my first Soranese nickname I felt some affinity to Antonio Borsetti and his wife Topa, and I was eager to find out more about them. Topo Borsetti was remembered by only a few people as a funny little man who did odd jobs around town, much as Carlone, the idiot savant, does nowadays. His appearance, and his activities of gathering, storing, and delivering—much like a pack rat—engendered his alias. He lived with Topa at the Poggio ("hill" in Italian), a neighborhood at the highest point of the abandoned side of the old town. The area for many years was also known as Stalingrado, because the town Communists held their meetings in a room there. Two of the women I interviewed, Matilde and Assunta, and their families were neighbors up at the Poggio around the same time. Jolly red-faced Chorchi, who died a couple of years after I came to Sorano and who looked remarkably like Winston Churchill, also was brought up at the Poggio. Chorchi's father, Biaggio Rossi, was a contemporary of Topo. Biaggio's wife, "La Biaggia," was the baker of Stalingrado.

Chorchi's brother happened to be known as Topanera. The story goes that on his wedding night he was so surprised by what was under his wife's skirts that he went around for days repeating in amazement, "*Che topa nera!*" What a black pussy! Nicknames were often passed on to sons, either because the name was particularly inventive or because the father was such a memorable character. Chorchi's nephew was long known as Figlio di Topanera, just as Michele, the ex-mayor, is still called Figlio di Canapino. The derivation of Michele's father's name was quite ordinary—his hair was the color of dried *canapa* (hemp)—but his reputation was not. He was a legendary ladies' man. My hair is also hemp-colored, and Michele amuses himself by sometimes calling me Canapino.

I could get little information about Topo and Topa, so I went up to the cemetery to locate their burial vaults. I quickly found Antonio Borsetti, who died in 1942. Whether or not he acted like a rat, he certainly looked like one, as evidenced by his photograph on the marble facing of his vault. I went on to find Genisio and Maria, the two Borsetti children, who both were in their early thirties when they died, and were entombed side by side. Try as I might, I could not find Topa, but I was soon distracted by other names and faces. I was drawn to a vault in a sheltered corner of the cemetery. Most of the flowers that adorn the vaults are dry or plastic, but this shelf had a vase with fresh fragrant gardenias, and a burning electric lamp in the shape of a flame. On the alabaster plaque was a photograph of Remo Crisanti, a tiny child who was born on February 9, 1978, and died the following day.

His surname jogged my memory of the story of another Crisanti, Adamo. I located Adamo Crisanti's chamber among the many who died during the Second World War. An epitaph is inscribed on the gray stone slab. *In the vigor of his twenty years, barbarously machine-gunned down by hostile hands just for blood lust on June 13, 1944. An innocent victim who in the hearts of all brings tears, and in those dear, anguish.* When returning from work as an electrician, Adamo was accosted by a band of Fascists. He was accused of being a member of the enemy partisans, the Partigiani, and then shot in the back. Particularly for townspeople his age, who although they had suffered deprivations were relatively immune to the violence of the war, Crisanti's death was a shocking event. The epitaph was signed by Adamo's brother, Romolo.

Romolo and Remo Crisanti, named after the mythical founders of Rome, were born to Alessina and Giovanni Crisanti in 1909. One brother perished shortly after his birth, and because no one could be sure which of the twins had died, the survivor was alternately called by the two names. Giovanni emigrated to the United States with another son shortly after the First World War, never to return. Alessina was abandoned and had to struggle to bring up her three remaining children. She also happened to be a great beauty, and went on to have two more children. The first, a daughter, was the result of a liaison with the town

priest. The second, Adamo, was the son of the mayor. The fathers did not acknowledge these two children, but their origins were known by all and must have caused consternation to some and amusement to others. Nevertheless, even today people are very reluctant to talk about the truth of Adamo and Alessina Crisanti, because the still-living legitimate children of the mayor are highly respected members of the community.

The mayor had not been elected but was nominated to the post by the Fascist government. He had the reputation of being brutal, liberally dispensing beatings and castor oil purges to all those who did not carry the Fascist membership card, or who were suspected of sympathizing with the Partigiani. The terrible irony is that his thugs ended up killing his own son.

Upon Alessina Crisanti's death in 1940, the thirty-one-year-old Romolo had his teenage half brother move in with him, his wife, and their two children. One of Romolo's boys, Alessandro, grew up and had two boys of his own. Alessandro named his second child Adamo, who currently works, as his great-uncle did, as an electrician. Romolo's other son is named Giovanni. Giovanni's firstborn was Remo, named for Romolo. Remo was the infant who died the day after he was born in 1978. Giovanni went on to have two more children, Anna who is studying medicine at the University of Siena, and a second Remo who is an undergraduate, also at Siena.

As I had not yet found Annunziata Borsetti, I returned to the cemetery on another occasion. I had learned from my auntie Annetta that Topa, after Topo's death, had moved to our side of town, just under my windows on the Via del Lato. She died in her apartment on May 14, 1964, a date Annetta happened to remember because it was the day her brother Ottorino was married. Nevertheless, I could not find Topa in the part of the cemetery where most of the people who died in the 1960s had been entombed. But sometimes a block of vaults, called *fornetti* in Italian, is bought by a family, or one *fornetto* is reserved in advance of an individual's death, so the dates are not so orderly, necessitating a thorough search of the whole cemetery.

I had just about given up, when I espied on old woman from the new town whom I only knew by sight. It was becoming quite dark and the low-voltage bulbs that light up the photographs, plaques, and flowers cast an unearthly glow in the cavern of fornetti. I seemed to smell burning incense, and was strongly reminded of an Indian market bazaar, strangely desolate. I walked over to where the woman was placing fresh flowers on a relation's fornetto, and explained that I was looking for Annunziata Borsetti. Her shawl had slipped from her head onto her shoulders, and wisps of her gray hair were blowing about in the swirling breeze. She stood back, almost in surprise, and demanded to know why I should be so interested in Annunziata. I simply said that I was doing research on old people in the town for a book I was writing. "Ah, tu sei l'americano." Upon identifying me she was not perturbed, and appeared to be satisfied with my explanation. She moved closer and put her hand confidentially on my forearm. "Annunziata was poisoned," she said. "Her body was removed from her fornetto to do an autopsy and was never returned. The person responsible, she whispered, "had from that time been given the nickname *La Spacciatrice*." The Pusher.

The story, as I was able to piece it together, was that Spacciatrice had been caring for the aged Topa in the apartment on the Via del Lato. Topa's health had declined, and she was to be moved to the casa di riposo, which cares for the infirm as well as the mentally ill. Spacciatrice had determined that Topa had quite a lot of money stashed away under her mattress, and so the night before Topa was to leave, Spacciatrice gave her an overdose of sleeping medication and made off with the money and other objects. Unfortunately, Topa was found dead the next morning, and everyone seemed to know who the villain was. Spacciatrice and an accomplice had been questioned and were to be taken away by the authorities. The frantic daughter of Spacciatrice went to Don Enzo, the priest, and said that if he did not intervene and save her mother, she would do herself harm. The outcome was that Topa's belongings were returned and the charges against Spacciatrice were dropped. Don Enzo resolved the dispute in the old way: He drew upon the power of an ethereal authority and found a solution within the community that was adequate for the aggrieved parties, and thus avoided a harsh legal remedy. Don Enzo undoubtedly made the best out of a bad situation, and the story made me realize that he had decidedly understated the degree of capacciolo madness he has endured.

In Italy the name of a deceased person usually is preceded by the word "poor"—*povera*. *La povera* Annunziata Borsetti is exceptionally poor. She was poisoned, robbed, and perhaps denied appropriate justice. Her sorry demise occurred almost forty years ago, so it is possible that the story was elaborated upon or perhaps even just made up. The fact is, however, that Topa, after she was disinterred for the autopsy, was lost.

I went for a stroll around the far side of town. Most of the haunting interiors have either collapsed or been torn down for safety's sake, leaving an ugly gash and empty, forlorn spaces. Other edifices were saved and rebuilt, the interiors redone and the doors replaced—the rooms no longer accessible for wandering through and dreaming in. Life has returned to the far side, in relatively small measure. The people that now occasionally inhabit it come from Germany, Denmark, the Netherlands, England, Switzerland, Brazil, Uruguay, the United States, and many of the big Italian cities. They have brought with them cement, iron, marble, new tiles, modern streetlamps—and different sensibilities. The streets are becoming orderly and sterile. The rubble has been removed, and many suggestive remnants of the past have been wiped away.

I came to the Poggio where Matilde, *povera* Assunta, *povero* Chorchi, *povero* Topanera, *povero* Topo, and *povera* Topa had all lived. I was able to walk for the first time down the Via della Rocchetta Vecchia, which, for as long as I had been in town, was impassable. At the bottom of the steps I stopped in front of a ground-level storeroom, the exterior walls of which were being renovated with new blocks of tufo and rows of new bricks. The original entrance had been lowered and constricted by a solidly built brick arch. Bricks had never been used in the original construction, and they look quite awful, but they apparently are the required materials to reinforce important weight-sustaining walls. As I walked away I got my bearings and realized that the storeroom had been the ruin of the bakery that the mysterious old widow had shown me some ten years before. She had brought the then derelict corner of Stalingrado to life for me, and was essentially responsible for inspiring me to inquire into Sorano's past. I had often thought of her, but no one in town could identify her. It suddenly occurred to me that the old widow could only have been Annunziata Borsetti, already dead twenty-five years by the time I met her. The wandering spirit of La Topa did not ask for revenge, but suggested paths, permitting me to form my own experiences and draw my own conclusions. I would like to think that some of the stories I have related might help her to rest in peace.

Perhaps, if we could examine the manners of different
nations with impartiality, we should find no people so
rude, as to be without any rules of politeness; nor any so
polite, as not to have some remains of rudeness.

BENJAMIN FRANKLIN[9]

As happened with my home in Sorano, the work of renovating my garden became all-consuming, and proved to be much more onerous than
I had imagined—particularly when I started acquiring other pieces of
land. Pulling out the roots of old-man's beard, bramble, and fig resulted
in the collapse of large portions of the dry wall that separates the two
terraces of the cocceria. Considering their size and length, some of
the dry walls that support the terraces surrounding Castel Vecchio,
built from large hand-hewn blocks of tufo, were impressive feats of
engineering. The cocceria's dry wall was a bit of a hodgepodge, thrown
up without much care and made of small irregular pieces of tufo inter-
spersed with boulders that had fallen from above. Building a new wall
might have been more practical than putting the old one back together.

Once the main dry wall was mended, I found other areas on the plot
that needed shoring up, so I set about trying to build other small-scale
walls. I knew that the eighty-year-old Domenico had worked in a tufo
quarry in his youth, before the advent of automation with diesel engines
and enormous spinning metal blades that cut the tufo into precise blocks.
He explained to me, over a bottle of Pum in Uncle Carlo's cantina one
afternoon, how to break up boulders of tufo with a heavy mallet, wedges,
and a triangle. It took me a frustrating while to master the technique, but
I ended up with enough fairly regular blocks to make my walls and steps.

The bank at the southern edge of the cocceria, which falls steeply to
the Etruscan path, had been supported in the long-ago past by a very
high dry wall, of which only a few blocks now remain. Later, black

---

[9] "Remarks Concerning the Savages of North America" (1784), as quoted in the
Zibaldone 4295

locust trees were introduced, as they were found to hold up banks with their long, intricate root systems. If neglected, however, the locusts can grow very tall and heavy, causing the landslides they were planted to prevent. My locusts were towering, so in the end I finished up with a pile of wood four times as big as the one I had made for Elidio and the Poisoner, and I opened up a magnificent view of Sorano from the top of the winding staircase to the far end of the terraces.

I have also thoroughly exposed my activities to critical view. Every day I'm asked by someone in town what I was so furiously hacking at or intently building. If not able to observe precisely what I'm doing, most people in town that have bothered to look simply remark, "*Lavori troppo, Americano.*" You are working too hard. Sometimes, if I go into the cool *Grotta della Topa* to lie on my hammock for a time, or disappear behind a boulder for too long, I can be accused of slacking off. I've begun to think that I'm constantly under surveillance, people fascinatedly watching me do things that would have been considered commonplace and uninteresting forty years ago. If I have visitors to the garden, people want to know who they were. One day Ivana came to visit, hobbling on her cane. After a wet spring, the grass was very high, and I was about to cut it. Ivana pointed out the self-seeded tall flowering arugula and various other edible plants mixed among the grass. She suggested that I make an omelet with poppies and a leafy green plant she called *ingrassa marito*— husband fattener. Melinda, a friend from the city of Lucca, identified the same plant as *ingrassa porci*—pig fattener. Perhaps the name indicates what Soranese women think of their husbands, but even if it is really only considered to be pig fodder in Lucca, it certainly tastes good.

Alberto recalled how, as a boy, he would come to the cocceria from the adjacent plot, where his cousin Eliseo's father kept pigs in one of the caves. With his friends he collected discarded ceramic tile from around the pottery, and then went back to Eliseo's plot and used the tiles with thin slivers of wood and seed as traps for songbirds. Alberto transportedly described cleaning the tiny birds of their feathers, sticking them on a spit with lumps of bacon fat, and slowly cooking them over hot coals. These were the pleasures of our uncomplicated and somewhat deprived youth, he explained. It was a long time since he had eaten songbirds, but he insisted that they are delicious. Alberto grew up to become mayor and, later, president of the province.

Once the terraces of the cocceria were cleaned and put in order, I began to think about what I wanted to plant there. With similar intent to creating a traditional home in town—being true to the past—I was contemplating making a native species garden. I soon realized that such a place would be impractical and certainly could not be representative of the type of gardens that had previously covered the hillsides surrounding Sorano. The black locust trees, introduced to stop erosion, are originally native to America's Southern Appalachian and Ozark Mountains. They are now considered a weed tree that crowds out some of the naturally occurring species, but in May the fragrant white flower clusters fill the valley with their lovely perfume, and are prized for dipping in batter and deep frying.

Shortly after the time when Edward Warren visited Sorano, many different foodstuffs and crops were introduced from the Americas via Britain, France, and Germany. Much of the arable land around Sorano had been devoted to growing wheat, but in the eighteenth century potatoes, corn, and tobacco began to be planted as well. There continued to be resistance to eating potatoes and corn in Tuscany, where they were thought of as animal feed. Giovanni Targioni Tozzetti, director of the Botanical Garden in Florence, a man of considerable influence in mid-eighteenth-century Florentine society, and great-grandfather of the woman who broke Leopardi's heart, suggested that priests experiment with planting potatoes in their parish gardens, in the hope that farmers would follow their example and begin to cultivate them.[10] With the ascension of the Lorena (Lorraine) family to power in Tuscany, food like German potato dumplings was introduced to the Florentine table, and was slowly integrated into the Tuscan diet.[11] Nowadays polenta, made from ground maize, and *gnocchi di patate* are staples of Italian cuisine.

Tomatoes, too, came from America, and they became essential to Italians long before Americans began to appreciate them. Because the

---

[10] Rossano Pazzagli, *Un Parroco "Agronomo" nella Toscana del Settecento* (Pisa: Ed. ETS, 1998)

[11] Eric Cochrane, *Florence in the Forgotten Centuries, 1527–1800* (Chicago: University of Chicago Press, 1976), p. 438

English thought tomatoes were poisonous, they were not widely eaten in the United States until the end of the nineteenth century. Hemp, which was originally from the Far East, was also intensively cultivated. Today it is banned, but in the eighteenth century it was as popular in Italy as it was in the burgeoning United States. Betsy Ross made her first Stars and Stripes out of hemp cloth. When Sorano was liberated between June 13 and 14, 1944, at the end of the Second World War, Gino Agostino's mother was expecting the soldiers to be Americans, and so she made a flag, also out of hemp, to greet them. Although she got the colors right, she confused the design, as she actually made a version of a British Union Jack. Ironically, the liberators were Moroccan Goumier auxiliary troops fighting for French commanders.

Liberation flag. Sorano. June 14, 1944

One of the first Lorena followers to arrive in Florence in the mid-eighteenth century was a man from Switzerland by the name of Castelmur. His business was coffee, a drink that was unknown at the time in Italy. He opened a café that became a very popular gathering point for Lorena partisans. Many Florentines deeply resented the new Granduca Francesco Stefano di Lorena and his cadre of foreigners, who had taken over the running of Florence, and so refused to go to the café and drink the coffee. Thus the use of coffee became a "declaration of ideological belief."[12] The popularity of coffee soon overrode principles, and the *caffè* became the focal point of Italian society. Today in Sorano the main piazza has the three bars, often identified by the political persuasions of their clientele, where current events are always being debated. I tend to go to the center right-wing bar, perhaps because of the lovely outdoor pergola that in spring is covered in cascading wisteria blossoms, under which I can sit and read the morning paper in relative peace. I must admit, however, that the best *caffè macchiato* is made up at the Fascist bar.

Even before I acquired my own garden, I had introduced some of the local farmers to sweet American corn on the cob slathered with butter, Long Island "beefsteak" tomato sandwiches, Georgia peanuts, and Yukon Gold potatoes. In return I have a steady supply of fresh vegetables. The heat of the cocceria is intense and certainly ideal for drying clay pots, so until I get around to building a large cistern to store water, and as long as my friends continue to give me their extra zucchini and *insalata,* I will not be planting a vegetable garden.

At the top of the rebuilt dry wall, I saved three old straggly grapevines. Uncle Carlo is of the opinion that they are original Grechetto vines that, because of the cocceria's relatively removed location, were unaffected by the phylloxera insect that devastated vineyards throughout Europe. Phylloxera was one of the scourges that came with the vast numbers of plants imported into Europe from America in the mid-nineteenth century. By grafting European vines onto phylloxera-resistant American rootstock, the problem was overcome, but it has always been thought by Europeans that the quality of the wine suffered as a result. Carlo provided me with several cuttings from his own vineyard, where he is certain that he has original European vines. I made deep holes, put the three-foot-long cuttings in the fertile ground, and they have wondrously all formed shoots. I will train the vines over the pergola I have yet to reconstruct, and I look forward to tasting the fruits in a couple of years' time.

The many spaces in the rebuilt dry wall have been filled with a

---

[12] Indro Montanelli and Roberto Gervaso, *L'Italia del Settecento* (Milan: Rizzoli, 1970), p. 283

selection of flowering rock plants that are hardy enough to survive the relative extremes of the cold wet winters and the heat and dryness of summer. All the plants came from local Italian nurseries, but a few originally hail from the mountains of the Balkans, the Rockies of America, and the deserts of Australia. I sharply pruned the neglected peach, apricot, apple, and plum trees that had been mostly smothered by old-man's beard, and I have planted a pear, an almond, three wild cherries, a flowering dogwood, and a pair of Kwanzan ornamental cherry trees. I dug up some small shrub oaks that had seeded themselves on the Etruscan path, and moved them to a specially cleared spot. Perhaps in my lifetime they will begin to resemble the twisted and gnarled centuries-old trees seen standing solitary in the middle of fields or by roadsides. In one corner I found a sad, neglected sage plant that with a little attention has rapidly flourished into a sprawling bush. I transplanted some wild fennel and added rosemary, thyme, and other culinary and medicinal herbs. Another corner I will keep wild, so I will always have the *ingrassa marito* and other edible plants and wildflowers at hand.

One shrub that is indigenous and common to all the countries of the Mediterranean, but that appears as far north as Scotland, is the *ginestra*. The long, slender branches were used in broom making, thus its English name, "broom." Ginestra thrives on dry banks and is one of the first plants to take over abandoned plots of land. In the spring the densely growing shrubs become a mass of pealike fragrant blossoms that color the hills surrounding Sorano with patches of bright yellow. In the past the flexible branches were used in the vineyards to tie up grapevines, and a few old men in town continue to harvest the branches in the fall, selecting the longest and collecting them in bundles to be left in the sun to dry, ready for use the following year. Ginestra had not appeared at the cocceria, so in summer I gathered some pods and scattered the seeds where I want them to grow. The plant was introduced to the United States and Australia in the late nineteenth century, and in those countries it is considered to be a highly invasive weed that should be eradicated. In Europe the lovely, tough, and resistant plant was adopted by kings. Henry II of England, by drawing on the French appellation *genêt* and the medieval term *Planta genista*, derived the name

Plantagenet for his family, and the noble weed first appears on the Great Seal of Henry's son, Richard the Lionheart.

Giacomo Leopardi lived his last days in a town near Naples, suffering terribly from rheumatism, severe asthma, and a broken heart. There on the barren flanks of Mount Vesuvius he pondered and wrote a poetic testament, published posthumously, to the "gentle *ginestra*, who with your fragrant thickets, make beautiful this spoiled and wasted land."

> ...Now all around,
> One ruin spreads,
> Wherein you take root, noble flower,
> As if in pity for the pain of others,
> And send the sweetest fragrance to the skies,
> Making the wasteland content. Now let him come
> And view these slopes, whose wish it is to praise
> Our mortal state; here he may gaze and see
> How loving Nature serves
> Our human race, and learn to value
> The power of man,
> Whom the cruel nurse, even when he fears it least,
> With the slightest motion can partly destroy,
> And may, with one slightly greater than the last,
> Suddenly and with no warning
> Wholly annihilate.
> Rendered upon these flanks
> Is that magnificent
> Progressive destiny of Humankind...

> ...You then
> Will bend your innocent head, unresisting
> Beneath the mortal strike;
> Neither bowed down, vain and cowardly,
> Before your future oppressor;
> Nor lifted in mad pride towards the stars,
> Or above the desert which

Was your home and birthplace,
Not by choice, but chance;
But wiser still, and less
Fallible than man, you do not think
Your fragile kind can be made immortal
By yourself, or fate.

FROM "LA GINESTRA, OR THE FLOWER OF THE DESERT" (1836)

Being subject to incursions, invasions, transplantations, natural calamities, and pestilence, the makeup of Sorano has altered over the town's history. Carlo the mechanic, with his long curly red locks; the tall, blonde, blue-eyed, and fair-skinned brother-and-sister postal carriers; and Giorgio the plumber's pug nose, freckles, red beard, and stocky build, all belie the impression that the town's people are of common stock, all descended from Bronze-Age cave-dwelling Villanovan ancestors. The faces and physiques of Sorano in fact reflect Italy's rich and calamitous past.

The Etruscans who ruled over the area of modern Tuscany from approximately 1000 BC to 500 BC are thought to have immigrated to the Italian peninsula from Asia Minor. The Romans, who were originally indigenous Villanovans, assimilated and destroyed the Etruscan people and their culture. Rome fell in 476 AD to the "barbarian" Germanic Ostrogoths, and Theodoric was named king of Italy in 493. The twenty-year Greco-Gothic War, which was terribly destructive to Italy, pitted the Greek and Armenian Byzantines against the Goths. The rule of the victorious Byzantines was short-lived, as another barbarian invasion resulted in the Italian Kingdom of the Lombards, a people originally from Scandinavia. In 573 most of the cities of Tuscany were occupied by the Greeks after their conquest of Rome, but by 592 the

Lombard Duke Ariulfo had conquered the area around Sorano.[13] With the Lombards came hundreds of thousands of settlers. Although the Lombards were to fall to the forces of the French Charlemagne in 774, they maintained duchies in Spoleto and Naples and were founders of the Aldobrandeschi family, who ruled over Sorano for 450 years.

Like many of the knights of the Crusades, Simon de Montfort passed through Italy on his way to the Christian Holy Land. Newly wedded to Eleanor Plantagenet, the sister of King Henry III of England, he stopped in Rome to make penance to Pope Gregory IX, who was angered because Eleanor had, by marrying Simon, broken a vow of chastity to her deceased former husband. Simon went on to so distinguish himself in Palestine that he was nominated to become viceroy of the Latin Kingdom of Jerusalem. Later, when King Louis IX of France was himself on crusade, Simon was asked by the French magnates to serve as regent in the king's absence. He refused and went on to assume the earldom of Leicester in England. He ultimately captured his brother-in-law King Henry III at the Battle of Lewes in 1264, established England's first Parliament, and ruled the country for one year.

Guy de Montfort was a son of Simon de Montfort and Eleanor Plantagenet. He was exiled from England after his father's death, and subsequently served as imperial vicar of Tuscany, representing Charles of Anjou, younger brother of Louis IX of France. The Italianized Carlo d'Angiò had been crowned king of Naples and Sicily by Pope Clement IV in 1266 and was the most powerful leader in Italy at the time, having sovereignty over key cities in Tuscany as well. For the sake of a beneficial military alliance, Count Ildebrandino "*il Rosso*" (the Red) Aldobrandeschi arranged to marry his only child, Margherita, to King Carlo's representative. Before Guy de Montfort avenged his father's death by killing his cousin Henry of Almain at the then papal city of Viterbo and escaped to Norway, he had two daughters with Margherita—offspring of the nephew to the Plantagenet King Henry III and the last of the Lombard Aldobrandeschi family. In 1293 Anastasia de Montfort was married at age eight to Romano Orsini of

---

[13] Gaspero Ciacci, *Gli Aldobrandeschi nella Storia e nella Divina Commedia* (Rome: Biblioteca d'Arte Editrice, 1935), p. 29

the powerful Roman family, just a year after Margherita had herself married an Orsini, following Guy's death in 1291,thus assuring the succession of Sorano and the Aldobrandeschi domains to the "little bears," the English translation of the family name. An enormous marble coat of arms representing the union, set above the entrance to Sorano's fortress, shows Aldobrandeschi lions conjoined by Orsini roses. One cannot help thinking that if Guy had not been so rash, the roses might instead have been *ginestra*.

Just as the Aldobrandeschi family produced a pope, Gregory VII, originally named Ildebrando and born five miles from Sorano, the Orsini had as their papal benefactor Giovanni Gaetano. Although he was pope for only three years, from 1277 to 1280, Nicholas III managed to so enrich his family that they became the most powerful Roman family of that period, and Sorano became their key defensive bulwark against the Republic of Siena. Dante subsequently condemned Pope Nicholas, like Guy de Montfort, to Hell: Accused of simony and nepotism, Nicholas is thrust headfirst into the fissured rock of the Malebolge, his writhing calves and feet aflame. "Then know that I was vested with the great mantle of power; a son who truly came out of the she-bear, I longed so much to advance the cubs that filling my purse was my great aim."[14]

During the fifteenth century, Sorano was often at war and twice under long siege. Ezra Pound in *The Cantos* writes of the siege of 1454, led by the ruthless mercenary Sigismondo Malatesta. Pound refers to Sorano as a lump of tufo "with pigs in the basements," and imagines a correspondence from the Orsini count to Sigismondo. "Siggy, darlint, wd. you not stop making war on insensible objects, such as trees and domestic vines, that have no means to hit back..." Malatesta was a model for Machiavelli's *The Prince*, and it is thought that his last name was originally a family nickname meaning "bad head." For the people of Sorano, bombarded from the surrounding hills, he certainly was a headache. I have a small travertine catapult ball on the mantle of one of my fireplaces, which may well have been launched by Malatesta's soldiers from somewhere near my garden.

---

[14] Dante Alighieri, *Inferno* Canto XIX, Trans. Robert Pinsky

The Orsini continued to war with others and among themselves. The family was torn apart by fighting among brothers and between sons and fathers, and in 1604 Sorano passed formally under the jurisdiction of the Medici family. The last years of the Medici were a time of decadence and decline, and nowhere was that felt more than in the area around Sorano. The low-lying plains of the Maremma were in a particularly bad state. The wars of previous centuries, political instability, and economic stagnation had led to the abandonment of lands. The lack of simple maintenance of the dense grid of channels and canals caused flooding and further loss of land. By the time the Lorena family took over from the Medici, the breadbasket of Tuscany was producing one-fourth the amount of grain it had grown at the beginning of the 1600s.[15] Whereas the population of the Maremma was approximately 200,000 in the thirteenth century, by 1739 it had only 25,000 inhabitants.[16] In the early 1740s, Edward Warren made a tour of the fortresses of Tuscany and noted that at one fortified coastal tower in the Maremma, at the center of a vast and stagnant swamp, the troops had *"l'aria di essere sempre malate"*—the air of being always ill. It was assumed that the "bad air" (*mal aria*) of the increasingly barren plains caused the considerable decline in population, but in fact conditions of poverty and the mosquito-borne disease malaria were the real causes. Deaths due to malaria were not confined to the rural poor, however. Cosimo de' Medici's Spanish wife, Eleonora de Toledo, and two of his sons are thought to have succumbed to the disease.[17]

Although Warren was responsible for the disarming and evacuation of Sorano's fortress, as it was no longer considered to be of strategic importance, it is likely that his further recommendations affected the Granduca's decision to send about one thousand German-speaking Lorrainer colonists to farm abandoned plots around the town. Apparently the number of colonists had dwindled by 1769, either assimilated or departed, but they were yet another infusion of foreign blood to Sorano that so vividly can be seen in today's faces.

---

[15] Danilo Barsanti, "La Toscana dai Medici ai Lorena. Vicende politiche e rinnovamento dello stato," in *Bollettino della Società storico maremmana* 47–48 (1984): 11–83
[16] Cochrane, *Florence in the Forgotten Centuries*, p. 357
[17] Franco Borsi, *L'Architettura del Principe* (Florence: Giunti Martello, 1980)

At my garden with Sorano always spread out before me, I'll sometimes pause, sit in my wicker chair, and consider the town. During its long history the physical aspect of Sorano has remained essentially the same, although the incredible vicissitudes of history have resulted in an unexpected mixing of peoples. Nevertheless, the vast majority of the unprivileged townspeople lived as they had for centuries. The recent changes to Sorano reflect the increasingly rapid progress that the developed world is undergoing, but when understood within the context of history, even the abandonment of Sorano and now the arrival of foreigners from all over the world somehow seem more natural. The concern is to instill somehow a respect and understanding for the past, so that some of the more unfortunate consequences of modernization can be avoided.

One day I had lunch, as I often do, with Annetta. I had asked her for some more information about the family of Adamo Crisanti. I went on to talk wonderingly about the details of Adamo's life and the lives of some of the other characters I have learned about. "*Ogni famiglia ha la sua storia,*" said Annetta. Every family has its own story. "You could not understand this because you are so disconnected from your family and your past," she went on. It occurred to me later that afternoon that I have now lived in Sorano longer than any other place, and I know more about several families in town than I do about my own. I went back to Annetta and told her about my thoughts. "*Eh beh, a questo punto sei Soranese, e communque tu sei come mio figlio.*" So? By now you are from Sorano, and anyway you are just like the son I never had.

Annetta has fed, helped, advised, and sometimes maddened me, much as my own mother has. Others in town, like Uncle Carlo and Michele, treat me without regard to my origin and as they would their good friends or family. It is fourteen years since I chose to settle in Sorano, and for the better part of that time I have worked hard on renovating my property, and later my garden, to the exclusion of most everything else. I have come to know the town much better than any other. Sitting back in my wicker chair outside the *Grotta della Topa*, I had to agree with Annetta. I can now finally say that I have a home, and it is Sorano.

SORANO 2002

All the Noise of It ~ 165

Where are Elmer, Herman, Bert, Tom and Charley,
The weak of will, the strong of arm, the
clown, the boozer, the fighter?
All, all are sleeping on the hill.
One passed in a fever,
One was burned in a mine,
One was killed in a brawl,
One died in a jail,
One fell from a bridge toiling for children and wife—
All, all are sleeping, sleeping, sleeping on the hill.
"The Hill," from *Spoon River Anthology* by Edgar Lee Masters[18]

Afterword

In 1988 there were some two hundred residents of the old town, and they were primarily born and bred in Sorano. As I have related, I was one of the first foreigners to come to Sorano, and had within four years bought three apartments that would have housed as many as twenty-five people only fifty years before. Three years ago, I had the opportunity to buy another apartment, which happily results in my now owning all the property at the end of my lane—the Via della Sparna. This was the same apartment that I had arranged for Matilde Rossi, one of my interviewees, to sell to a Neapolitan woman twenty years ago—much to the wrath of my neighbor Annetta. In 2013 I paid almost twice as much for that one forty-square-meter apartment as I did for the rest of my two-hundred-square-meter home in the late 1980s and early '90s.

In the last several years I have also expanded my land in the valley from the original two allotments I purchased at the beginning of the millennium, so that I now have a total of seven plots that in 1900

---
[18] Edgar Lee Masters, *Spoon River Anthology* (New York: Macmillan, 1915)

would have supported seven different families. In total I have about one hectare, and on the land I have created a botanic garden, fruit orchard, vegetable patch, and sculpture garden, where I exhibit some of my ceramic sculptures. Again in 1988, there were still a few people from Sorano who tended their plots. There were two vineyards, an olive orchard, and five or six vegetable gardens. Nowadays, when I look out my window I see a largely wooded landscape, and my garden is the only one discernable. One hundred years before, there would have been very few trees, and the view would have been of landscaped gardens.

One of the great advantages to acquiring all my land is that I am able to harvest plenty of oak, maple, elm, and black locust, and that resulted in a very satisfactory change at home: I bought a wood-fired stove, on which I cook and which heats my radiators, and so replaced my oil-fired boiler. On the land I have discreetly installed solar panels that provide power for my caves and the ceramic studio I have made there.

At this writing it has been twenty-eight years since I arrived in Sorano. On my first night I was put up in a spartan room in the old Jewish ghetto with only a bed frame, a lumpy mattress, and a rather greasy coarse woolen blanket. It was cold, I felt decidedly like an ascetic monk, and I did not sleep well. It turns out that I was in the room where an important Catholic cardinal, Angelo Comastri, was born on September 17, 1943. The night I slept there was his birthday. So I have always felt an odd closeness to Cardinal Comastri. That room is also above, and in the same building as, my first apartment, which I was to buy only two months later.

As the years went by, I never attended Mass, although I did become quite friendly with the town priest. Don Enzo arrived as a dashing young man on his Moto Guzzi motorcycle in the early 1950s and served the people of Sorano for sixty years. He was a keen amateur archaeologist, and whenever he came upon some reliquary or other objects—a presumed Della Robbia terracotta glazed figure of the Madonna and child, for example—he would have me photograph it. Upon his retirement I was moved when he presented me with an old ceramic *ziro* for storing olive oil, made by one of the local Porri family of potters.

Don Enzo was replaced by the very jovial Don Tito. We hit it off because we both enjoy cooking. Sorano was quite famous for its Good

Friday procession, and it was to be Tito's first. The previous year the annual event was jeopardized when a wine fortified Christ was on the cross. He was so inebriated that Don Enzo had to feed him his lines. When Christ famously proclaims, "Ho sete"—I am thirsty—someone clever in the crowd below piped up, to much hilarity, "do you want red or white?" To add injury to insult, Christ then passed out, slumped forward, and he and the cross came crashing down. Christ was relatively unharmed, but Don Enzo was so incensed that he insisted the procession be canceled the following year.

Via del Ghetto

Don Tito invited me for pizza, which he made in his home wood-fired oven, and surprised me by asking that I play Christ in that year's passion play. Perhaps hoping to assuage Don Enzo's ire and wanting to make a fresh start, Tito thought it appropriate to ask an "outsider" to assume the role. Feeling awkward about disappointing Tito, I agreed. The preparations were somewhat more complicated than I expected, particularly as Cardinal Comastri's cousin Arturo was directing the extravaganza. I had seen the procession in past years, with Christ carrying the cross through the streets and then being tied up on it, but I was not aware that Arturo this particular year wanted to give Christ a much more significant speaking role. I was required to memorize pages of text lifted from the screenplay of Franco Zeffirelli's *Jesus of Nazareth*. It went off without a hitch, and I was successfully crucified.

Another one of my nicknames in town comes from the event—Cristo, or the playfully pejorative "Cristaccio." Even a few years later, if ever Donatello sees me in the piazza he will yell out, "Cristaccio Morto!"—Nasty Dead Christ—and, to general amusement, I respond by thrusting my arms out to my sides. The Good Friday performance was videotaped by one of the national news programs because I was supposedly the first American ever to play Christ in a small Italian town procession. I was told that Cardinal Comastri approved.

Cardinal Comastri is one of the most senior cardinals in the Church hierarchy and was assistant to, and very close to, both Pope John Paul II and Pope Benedict XVI. Upon Benedict's resignation, it was thought by some that Comastri was the frontrunner to become the next pope. In Sorano we were praying that Sorano's native son would win out—if only to bring the town some notoriety and pilgrims to my doorstep—but it was not to be. Ironically, Sorano has become famous just this last year, particularly in the United States, because of a Fiat 500 television ad filmed in the town and featuring a tablet of Viagra that ricochets off the church bells, falls into the gas tank, and transforms the car into a muscular SUV. It was voted best Super Bowl commercial in several online polls.

After only five years Don Tito gave way to Don Fabio, a rather intense fellow who invited me to his quarters to look at his clearly suggestive photographic collection of lighthouses, which he had snapped while visiting Ireland some years before. I declined the invitation, made a quick escape up to one of the bars, and told my story of the man I dubbed *Don Faro* (Don Lighthouse). Many people in Italy have difficulty pronouncing *r*, and they are said to speak with an "erre moscia"—a soft *r*. Thus *faro* becomes *fallo*, which in English means both "mistake" (or even sin) and "phallus." Pronounced this way, the name caused quite some hilarity, and it became his nickname. Unlike Don Tito, who increased his flock by attracting people with his wonderful meals in the church square, Don Faro cultivated the company of young boys—he was also a Boy Scout leader—and seemed quickly to alienate his congregation.

Don Faro was soon replaced by Padre Mario, a gregarious Italian who, after having spent many years as a missionary in Brazil, exhibited an ability for soccer—which made him popular with the kids—and a fondness for a certain married lady in town, which proved his downfall. Padre Mario departed suddenly, and upon his heels arrived Don Felicien, originally of the Belgian Congo. He joins Don Egbetongbo—appropriately known as Don Togo (his country of origin), the priest of the nearby town of Sovana. One of Egbetongbo's predecessors in Sovana was Hildebrand, who in 1073 became Pope Gregory VII. Ildebrando's name was likely derived from his pagan Longbeard relations. The Germanic Longobards swept into Tuscany in the sixth century and established the Duchy of Tuscia as part of the Lombard Kingdom of Italy. Ildebrando is known for having twice excommunicated Henry IV, King of the Germans and Holy Roman Emperor. Gregory VII was subsequently canonized for his good works and has an impressive Etruscan tomb in Sovana named after him, the *Tomba Ildebrando*.

Since the end of the Second World War, outside of Florence, there has been a relatively gentle influx of Americans, British, and Germans to Tuscany. The gradual British invasion has resulted in the Tuscan region of Chianti being facetiously dubbed Chiantishire. I was one of the first foreigners to arrive in the far less known southern Tuscan township of Sorano—and that was in the 1980s. Generally, I and other expats came because of a love of Italian culture, food, wine, and lifestyle—la dolce vita. However, particularly since the fall of the Berlin Wall in 1989, the breakup of the Soviet Union, the expansion of the European Union, and general globalization, there have been profound and fast demographic changes to the towns of Tuscany.

I remembered talk in the mid-1990s of two Romanians who had come to Sorano and taken work at one of the local volcanic tufo quarries. The work is physically very demanding and pays poorly; it is certainly not what most young Italians aspire to nowadays. Nor do Italians want to devote themselves to the Church—thus the five resident Indian nuns and the resident priests from the Congo and Togo. I'll often see idle Italian youths at the bars, basically just waiting for a break to get to Florence or Rome and seek their fortunes while living off of their doting parents' largesse. Over the last twenty years, those two hardworking Romanians have brought family and friends to Sorano, so that Romanians now, according to the latest census, officially number about a hundred residents out of a total of some 3,500 in the township of Sorano. Most of them live in the town of Sorano, the population of which is now only about 800 people. So basically one-eighth of the population of this sleepy out-of-the-way medieval Tuscan hilltown is now Romanian. They work as builders, and some have even started their own building companies. Their wives and daughters clean homes and care for the elderly. Two Romanian sisters recently bought out the one remaining general food store in the old town and in addition to local products also sell Romanian sausages and wine.

Twenty kilometers from Sorano is the larger and better known Tuscan hilltown of Manciano. It is surrounded by vast estates owned by wealthy Italians and is very near to the world-renowned spa town of Saturnia and the exclusive seaside town of Capalbio with its summer homes of VIP politicians, musicians, and actors—places that most Europeans and Americans only dream about visiting. However, Romanians were more than happy to pick tomatoes and grapes and olives for work, and now apparently make up nearly a quarter of the population of the town of Manciano—unofficially it may be as many as one-half—and there are two general stores in Manciano that sell exclusively Romanian food products.

One of the ironies about the Romanians is that they have little interest in things Italian. They are here to make money, and perhaps would like eventually to return to Romania. They keep to themselves and are not particularly interested in Italian food, culture—or music, for that matter. There are now really only three people who cultivate gardens in the Lente River valley below Sorano: myself, a man from Mestre, and a Romanian who has a small plot with a snarling dog on a chain, chickens, and piles of collected wood and other scavenged items. On weekends he'll have large gatherings for barbecues, and I find it disconcerting when my previously silent contemplation of the extraordinary view of Sorano from my garden is interrupted by loud, jangling Romanian gypsy/pop music.

The second most represented nation in Sorano is Morocco. A few years after I arrived, a Moroccan man married a bar owner in Elmo—another local town, five kilometers distant and still within the township of Sorano. As with the Romanians, his family and friends soon followed, and there are now officially ninety Moroccans living primarily in the towns of Sorano and San Quirico di Sorano. Censuses began to be taken in the township of Sorano in 1861 when there was a population of 4,473 Italians. By 1921 the population had increased to nearly 8,500. Since then the population has declined—most precipitously around the time of the forced evacuation of the far side of Sorano in the 1950s and '60s. The figure for the latest census is about 3,400 residents.

Lately the town has been offering incentives to settle in Sorano, to increase the tax base so as to maintain essential services, but also to insure that adequate funds continue to come in from the provincial capital of Grosseto and the region of Tuscany. There had been concern that grades in the local school might have to be combined, or that the school would be closed altogether because of a lack of children. In 1861 Italy had 38.3 births per 1,000 people. There are now only 8.4 births per 1,000 people. Moroccan women produce an average of about 2.2 children, considerably more than Italian women. Moroccans have been offered residency, free public housing, healthcare, and education in Sorano, and recently they have established a mosque in the town of San Quirico—eight kilometers from Sorano. They are also able to automatically convert their Moroccan driver's licenses into Italian ones, which is necessary as most of the males seem to be itinerant peddlers.

It is not so easy for Americans, however, to get licenses or even maintain residency in Italy. I had to make a few trips to the United States to gather the required documents to apply for an "elective residency" visa, meaning that I did not intend to apply for work, nor did I need any state assistance in Italy. Every year, I had to drive ninety minutes to the provincial capital and stand on line for hours, mostly with foreigners applying for work permits, whereas I was simply renewing my permit to stay in Italy. Oftentimes when there were too many people, we were simply turned away and told to come back the next day. One year I became extremely annoyed by this process and had words with the town clerk. She responded by saying, "You, Christopher, as an American are a foreigner and no better than someone from the Congo, so you must follow the rules. In fact for me you are a Congolese." This story was greeted with delight at the bar, and was the origin for yet another one of my nicknames—"Il Congolese." I have yet to tell Don Felicien, the new town priest, that we are countrymen.

Upon eventually being granted residency status I was then required to get an Italian driver's license within a year. Unlike with Morocco, Italy does not have an agreement with the United States. So despite learning from African rally drivers as a teen, and driving all over the world (twenty of those years in Italy), I was obligated to attend Drivers School and take the written exam and practical driving test, all at considerable cost. Still annoyed about the continued residency requirements, I had another argument with the town clerk. This time she was offended, and punished me by canceling my residency, which was a blessing in disguise as she actually saved me the hassle of having to get my driver's license. Nevertheless, her action created a host of other problems. When I next flew into Milan, I was denied entry by an immigration official because I had, as an American nonresident, exceeded my maximum stay of three months in one year.

It has become increasingly apparent that the goodwill that existed towards the United States after the Second World War has been totally undermined by the havoc unleashed in the Middle East by the two Bush forays in Iraq. My only solution was to draw upon my half-English heritage, and I finally became a British citizen. I then went back to

Sorano and the decidedly unamused town clerk and demanded residence as a member of the European Union. She could not refuse. People have stopped addressing me as L'Americano. My newest nickname is "L'Inglese." The Englishman. Nevertheless, I recall now that my most curious nickname in Sorano came after the September 11 attack in New York in 2001. For months thereafter, people called me "Torre Gemelli"—Twin Towers. But for most of the years I have spent in Italy I have been—and still am, for that matter—an American.

Having been born in 1960, I was twenty-eight when I bought my first apartment in Sorano. In 1988 there were two general stores—one an emporium that was a treasure trove of old Italian housewares, toys, and assorted knickknacks. There was a hardware store, two food stores, and the old apothecary, with floor-to-ceiling fitted wooden cabinets and a lovely assortment of glass apothecary jars—clear, amber, and green— with their contents written in a florid old script. There still were a few dozen elderly inhabitants who were my neighbors, who welcomed me into their homes and patiently taught me Italian, cooking, some of the old ways—and brought the even-then relatively barren streets to life for me. Having recently completed some graduate study of anthropology, I used the tools and techniques that would be used to write an ethnography. I conducted interviews with my "native informants" and fortunately recorded most of them, so I was able to go back a few years later when I spoke Italian reasonably fluently to understand much better what I had been told. You have read some of those accounts here.

By 1998 a few of my friends had passed away. I was inspired not only by the death of Marietta Savelli, but also that of my own father in 1996, to compile these reminiscences and write a book of popular anthropology. I drew on some letters I had written to friends and family to bring myself into the story. And so came about the second iteration of *All the Noise of It*. My editor had wanted me to discuss my interest in Italian cookery, and although I couldn't see how to insert random recipes, this was the genesis of my second book, *Feasts from Paradiso*, which will be published in due course. *Feasts* takes place in the botanic garden I created and the Paleolithic caves that I have made habitable in the valley below Sorano. Sadly my editor died, but I did manage to sell *Feasts* to another publishing company. Shortly thereafter, the publisher, who particularly championed my second book, was fired, and *Feasts* was canceled. Somewhat demoralized, I put both books on the shelf, but after another ten years of further enriching experiences I decided to return to my first book.

Now, in 2016, all but one of my old friends have died. The eldest, Pietro Barbini, was born on Christmas Day in 1903 and died in May of 1991. Elidio Agnelli, who was so outraged when I cut a few small oaks on "his land" adjacent to mine in the valley below Sorano, was born on February 9, 1917. He forgave me only after several years. I was walking along the old Etruscan path that leads to my garden, and ran into him struggling with a large and heavy bundle of firewood. When I of-

Annetta Forti

fered to help him, he looked at me almost in shock and said that I was too good to be in Sorano and that I should not be nice to people who might have wronged me. The following day he presented me with his garden hoe and a folding chair that he would sun himself on, saying that he was too old to continue the climb to his garden. A short while later he died, on May 14, 2009. Assunta Mauciatti, a woman with an extraordinarily benevolent nature, who recounted that she was married with a black eye after coming to blows with her sister when grappling over the single cover they had to stay warm in the bed they shared, was born on August 28, 1916, and died on April 5, 1997.

Most of my other friends were born after the First World War and up through the 1920s. Alberto Mezzetti, who worked in the town hall, was born in March of 1921 and died at ninety-one in 2012. He invited me several times to his garden, where he made a fine red wine and a marvelous soppressata—headcheese—that my father particularly enjoyed many years before. Matilde Rossi, whose apartment I sold and then recently bought for myself, and who as a child during winter would wake up covered in snow, was born on the second of July, 1922, and died on the first of October in 2006. The youngest, Carlo Bizzi, the town plumber who taught me how to make wine, and whom I helped make his wine for twenty years, was born on the tenth of May in 1934, and died on the twelfth of July, 2008.

Annetta Forti was perhaps the person to whom I was closest. She was very much like my surrogate Italian mother, and was the sister of Marietta Savelli, whose funeral I wrote about. Annetta was a wonderful cook and taught me most of what I know about the Italian table. We had many meals together, and many rows, as she was a particularly hot-headed *capacciolo*. Although she thought me *"cattivo"*—wicked—at times, we invariably made up over a delicious bowl of *acquacotta* or a plate of her homemade *tortelli* with *ragu*. Annetta was still a very active eighty-eight-year-old when, one evening, she went into pulmonary arrest, and I rushed to her side and held her up in my arms, as she could not breathe while sitting. The emergency services arrived after almost an hour, without oxygen or a defibrillator, and she died before she should have. Nevertheless, she lived a long and full life. She was born on the ninth of April, 1924, and died on the thirteenth of October in 2012.

Twenty-eight years before I came to Sorano, when I was a newborn in 1960, the far side of town had not been condemned and the new town had not been built, so the approximately 3,000 Italian inhabitants still lived in the historical center—the old town. All of my friends were in the prime of their lives. Michele Sarti, who provided me with invaluable advice on dealing with Italian bureaucracy and was my primary source of historical information about the town, was then the town mayor. He was born on February 21, 1919, and died on the August 27 in 2008. After he was forced to close his pottery in the 1950s, Luigino Porri, the town potter, had moved to the coastal town of Orbetello, where he worked as a builder for many years. Upon retiring he returned to Sorano, just about the time that I first came, and started throwing pots on his wheel again. Also born in 1919, he died on November 11, 2011.

The changes that the old town of Sorano has undergone in the last fifty-six years have been astounding. Today there are fewer than fifty year-round inhabitants of the old town. In the ghetto, the old Jewish quarter of Sorano, several Romanians have rented houses, and I facetiously refer to it as Little Bucharest. In the new town, the area of housing that has been established for the growing Moroccan contingent is known as Little Casablanca. There are certainly still a few Italians here. Giuliano, a Florentine, preceded me in Sorano by some 10 years. We share a love of literature, and storytelling, and he has become a friend. Giuliano was a professor of Italian and recently we did a reading together at the local library of excerpts from Edgar Lee Masters' *Spoon River Anthology*—I in English and he in Italian. The collection of poetic epitaphs is one of Giuliano's favorites, and the stories of characters in turn-of-the-twentieth-century rural Illinois remind me of some of the curious, funny, and tragic stories I tell here. Massimo, the expert builder who poured my floors and did some other work for me, is now in his seventies and lives in the street below my home. He was born and bred here to parents from old Sorano, and I refer to him as "L'Ultimo Soranese." The last person from Sorano.

Considering what has happened in the past fifty-six years, it would be impossible to imagine what Sorano will be like twenty-eight years from now. All I can be sure of, if I'm still around, is that I will be eighty-four years old. I am sitting at my desk, looking across the valley at my garden as I write these words, and so I hope that my garden will not have been allowed to become overgrown again. I permitted myself to plant two exotic trees there. In the main botanic garden I planted an oriental Kwanzan cherry tree, which has such beautiful pink blossoms that I can see clearly from my windows in the spring. At the far end of my fruit orchard I planted a sequoia six years ago. It is now about twenty feet tall. In 2042 it will probably be beginning to tower above the other trees, and will be visible clearly from the town. Perhaps the Romanians and Moroccans and other people from wherever they may have come will point at the tree and remark—"You see, there once even was an American here."

Sorano 2016

About the Author

Christopher H. Warren is a writer, photographer, and artist. Grants from foundations, and assignments for the United Nations and other organizations led him to work in numerous developing-world countries. His photographs and articles have been published in journals, magazines, newspapers, and books, and his work has been exhibited in the United States, the United Kingdom, and Europe.